P9-CQV-606

The Best of Mr. Food®
Cookin' Quickies

"If you're looking for family-pleasin' recipes that don't take all day to make, you'll love my latest collection! The whole gang'll be beggin' for more!"

Cheesy Ziti Toss,
page 59

Black-and-Blue Salad, page 124

Chocolate-Raspberry Cake,
page 178

The Best of **Mr. Food**®

Cookin' Quickies

Oxmoor House®

©2002 by Oxmoor House, Inc.
Book Division of Southern Progress Corporation
P.O. Box 2262, Birmingham, Alabama 35201-2262

ISBN: 0-8487-2523-9
ISSN: 1534-5505

Printed in the United States of America
Ninth Printing 2007

Ginsburg Enterprises Incorporated
   Chief Executive Officer: Art Ginsburg
   Chief Operating Officer: Steven Ginsburg
   Vice President, Publishing: Caryl Ginsburg Fantel
   Vice President, Creative Business Development: Howard Rosenthal
   Vice President, Sales and Licensing: Thomas R. Palombo
   Director of Finance and Administration: Chester Rosenbaum

Oxmoor House, Inc.
   Editor-in-Chief: Nancy Fitzpatrick Wyatt
   Executive Editor: Susan Carlisle Payne
   Art Director: Cynthia R. Cooper
   Copy Chief: Catherine Ritter Scholl

THE BEST OF MR. FOOD® COOKIN' QUICKIES, featuring the recipes of Mr. Food, Art Ginsburg
   Editors: Allison Long Lowery, Kelly Hooper Troiano
   Copy Editor: Donna Baldone
   Editorial Assistant: Jane Lorberau Gentry
   Publishing Systems Administrator: Rick Tucker
   Director, Test Kitchens: Elizabeth Tyler Luckett
   Assistant Director, Test Kitchens: Julie Christopher
   Recipe Editor: Gayle Hays Sadler
   Test Kitchens Staff: Jennifer Cofield; Gretchen Feldtman, R.D.;
      David Gallent; Ana Kelly; Kathleen Royal Phillips; Jan A. Smith
   Senior Photographer: Jim Bathie
   Photographer: Brit Huckabay
   Senior Photo Stylist: Kay E. Clarke
   Photo Stylist: Ashley J. Wyatt
   Director, Production and Distribution: Phillip Lee
   Production Coordinator: Leslie Johnson
   Production Assistant: Faye Porter Bonner

   Contributors:
   Designer: Rita Yerby
   Indexer: Mary Ann Laurens

To order additional publications, call 1-800-765-6400.

For more books to enrich your life, visit **oxmoorhouse.com**

Cover: *Southwestern Burgers, page 72*

Contents

Welcome!!

"*Wouldn't you love to cut your kitchen time in half? You can with my newest collection of cookin' quickies that will help you get dinner on the table in no time. Easy-to-find ingredients, numbered cooking steps, and tips and secrets from my own kitchen make cooking a snap. And these recipes aren't just fast—they're also downright delicious! From appetizers for your next party, to everyday meals and decadent desserts, and everything in between, this collection promises a hit every time. You'll have picky eaters beggin' for seconds, guests raving, and the whole family craving more! 'OOH IT'S SO GOOD!!'*"

Mr. Food

Party Hearty

“Let the fun begin with these ooh-so-easy appetizers and beverages.”

Black-Eyed Peas con Queso

3 cups

½ cup butter
1 large onion, finely chopped
2 cloves garlic, pressed

1 (16-ounce) loaf process cheese spread, cubed
5 jalapeño peppers, unseeded and chopped (see tip below)
2 (15.8-ounce) cans black-eyed peas, drained

1 Melt butter in a large Dutch oven; add onion and garlic, and sauté until tender.

2 Add cheese, and cook over low heat, stirring constantly, until it melts. Stir in peppers and peas; cook, stirring often, until thoroughly heated. Serve with tortilla chips.

Spice It Up!
Bring good luck to your New Year with this spicy-hot dip that's brimming with cheese, jalapeños, and black-eyed peas. For more timid taste buds, you can tame the heat by seeding the jalapeño peppers before chopping them. Much of the heat hides in the seeds. Always wear rubber gloves when handling jalapeños, and keep your fingers away from your eyes for safety.

Spinach-Feta Dip

2 cups

2   (3-ounce) packages cream cheese,
        softened
1   clove garlic, minced
¾   cup crumbled feta cheese
1   tablespoon minced fresh dill or
        1 teaspoon dried dillweed
¼   teaspoon salt
⅛   teaspoon pepper
1½   cups finely chopped fresh spinach
        (see note below)

1   (8-ounce) container sour cream

1 Combine first 6 ingredients in a medium bowl, stirring until mixture is blended. Stir in spinach. Cover and chill at least 2 hours.

2 Stir in sour cream before serving. Serve with fresh vegetables or toasted pita wedges.

" This flavorful dip will be a hit at your next party. Whether you need an ooh-so-fancy accompaniment with a vegetable tray or a quick-and-easy dip for a last-minute party, you'll crave this creamy concoction. Find 10-ounce bags of fresh spinach in the produce section of the supermarket. Measure out what you need for this recipe, and save the rest for a healthy salad! "

BLT Dip

4 cups

1 cup mayonnaise
1 (8-ounce) container sour cream

1 pound bacon, cooked and crumbled
2 large tomatoes, chopped

1 Combine mayonnaise and sour cream in a medium bowl, stirring well with a wire whisk.

2 Stir in bacon and tomatoes. Serve immediately with melba toast rounds.

Mix It Up!

If you're a BLT fan, you'll love this versatile dip—it includes everything but the lettuce! For a spicier version, use salsa in place of the tomatoes. For a lighter version, use nonfat mayonnaise, fat-free sour cream, and turkey bacon. You'll even enjoy it over lettuce as a chunky salad dressing.

Fiery 'Fridgerator Jelly

3 half-pints

3 jalapeño peppers, seeded and
   coarsely chopped (see tip on
   page 10)
½ green bell pepper, coarsely chopped

3 cups sugar
½ cup cider vinegar
½ (6-ounce) package liquid fruit pectin
2 tablespoons fresh lime juice

1 Process jalapeños and bell pepper in a food processor until smooth.

2 Combine pepper purée, sugar, and vinegar in a nonaluminum saucepan. Bring to a boil over medium-high heat, stirring constantly. Boil 3 minutes; stir in pectin and lime juice. Boil, stirring constantly, 1 minute. Remove from heat, and skim off foam with a metal spoon.

3 Pour into hot, sterilized canning jars, filling to ¼" from top; wipe jar rims. Cover at once with metal lids, and screw on bands; cool. Store in refrigerator.

" I've skipped the canning process to make an easy, small batch of keep-in-the-fridge jelly. It's a cool appetizer with a sweet-hot flavor teaser. I love it served over cream cheese with crackers or toast, or with meats as a relish. It also makes a great gift for the holidays—just remember to tell 'em to keep it in the fridge!"

Shrimp 'n' Cheese Appetizer

4 to 6 appetizer servings

¼ pound cooked, unpeeled
medium-size fresh shrimp
(about 35 per pound)

¾ to 1 cup salsa
2 teaspoons chopped fresh cilantro
1 (8-ounce) package cream cheese,
softened
1 green onion, chopped

1 Peel shrimp, and devein, if desired; chop shrimp.

2 Stir together salsa and cilantro. Place cream cheese on a serving plate; spoon salsa mixture over cream cheese. Top with shrimp, and sprinkle with green onion. Serve with tortilla chips.

Time-Saver vs. Dime Saver

Save yourself some time and effort, and buy cooked, peeled shrimp from the seafood department of your supermarket to make this elegant appetizer even easier. But if you want to save at the checkout, start with ⅓ pound raw shrimp in the shell and boil it yourself—3 to 5 minutes in boiling salted water will do the trick.

Fiesta of a Spread

18 to 20 appetizer servings

1 (10½-ounce) package corn chips, crushed

¼ cup butter, melted

2 (16-ounce) cans refried beans

1 (1¼-ounce) package taco seasoning mix

1 (6-ounce) carton avocado dip

1 (8-ounce) container sour cream

3 (2¼-ounce) cans sliced ripe olives

2 tomatoes, seeded and chopped

2 (4.5-ounce) cans chopped green chilies, drained

1 (8-ounce) package Monterey Jack cheese with peppers, shredded

1 Preheat the oven to 350°. Combine crushed corn chips and butter; press into bottom and 1" up sides of a lightly greased 9" springform pan. Bake at 350° for 10 minutes. Cool on a wire rack.

2 Combine refried beans and taco seasoning mix, stirring well; spread over prepared crust. Layer avocado dip and remaining 5 ingredients over refried bean mixture; cover and chill 8 hours.

3 Place on a serving plate, and remove sides of springform pan. Serve with large corn chips or tortilla chips.

You might want to add a half pound shredded cooked chicken or browned ground beef to this popular Mexican spread for a hearty change. You can also substitute 1 cup homemade guacamole for avocado dip, if you enjoy making the creamy dip. Crushing the corn chips? No problem. Just transfer the chips to a zip-top bag, seal the bag, and have at it with a meat mallet or rolling pin.

Chili 'n' Cheese Popcorn

8 cups

2 (3.5-ounce) packages butter-flavored microwave popcorn

2 tablespoons Parmesan cheese
¼ teaspoon salt
⅛ teaspoon garlic powder
1 teaspoon paprika
½ teaspoon chili powder
Pinch ground red pepper

1 Prepare popcorn according to package directions.

2 Combine cheese and remaining 5 ingredients. Open popcorn bags carefully, and sprinkle cheese mixture into both. Close bags, and shake to coat. Serve immediately, or cool and store in an airtight container.

Movie Night!
Invite the whole gang over for movie night, and munch away on this pepped-up popcorn. The recipe makes lots, so you'll be ready for a double feature!

Roasted Bacon Pecans

2 cups

2   cups pecan halves
2   tablespoons butter, melted
6   bacon slices, chopped

2   tablespoons sugar
½   teaspoon salt

1 Preheat the oven to 350°. Stir together first 3 ingredients; spread in an ungreased 10" x 15" rimmed baking sheet.

2 Bake at 350°, stirring occasionally, 25 minutes or until pecans are toasted and bacon is done.

3 Sprinkle with sugar and salt; stir to coat. Cool pecans, and store in refrigerator.

"You may need to make 2 batches of these delicious snackers, and this recipe's super easy to double. I guarantee your guests won't be able to stop once they start nibbling on these toasted treats. You'll have 'em coming back for more, more, more!"

Blue Cheese Crisps

32 appetizers

½ cup butter, softened
1 (4-ounce) package crumbled blue
 cheese, softened
½ cup walnuts

1 baguette, cut into 32 slices (see
 note below)

1 Preheat the oven to 350°. Stir together er butter and blue cheese until blended; stir in walnuts. Set aside.

2 Place baguette slices in a single layer on baking sheets.

3 Bake at 350° for 3 to 5 minutes. Turn slices, and spread evenly with blue cheese mixture. Bake 5 more minutes. Serve immediately.

> " '*Baguette' is just a fancy name for French bread that's shaped into a long, narrow loaf. You can find freshly baked baguettes in the bakery section of your supermarket. The crispy crust and chewy inside make it perfect for these party starters!*"

Fried Mozzarella Sticks

18 cheese sticks

1 pound mozzarella cheese
½ cup all-purpose flour
¼ teaspoon salt
¼ teaspoon pepper
2 large eggs, lightly beaten
1 cup Italian-seasoned breadcrumbs

Vegetable oil

1 Cut mozzarella into 18 (3½" x ½") sticks. Combine flour, salt, and pepper. Dip cheese sticks into egg; dredge in flour mixture, and dip again in egg. Roll in breadcrumbs; press firmly so crumbs adhere. Place on wax paper, and chill 30 minutes.

2 Pour oil to a depth of 1" into a large heavy skillet; heat to 350°. Fry cheese sticks until golden; drain on paper towels. Serve immediately.

❝ I guarantee these kid-friendly snacks won't stay around for long. Serve 'em with marinara sauce for dipping, and sit back and enjoy the raves!❞

Phyllo Crab Shells

2½ dozen

½ pound fresh crabmeat

¼ cup sour cream
¼ cup mayonnaise
1½ teaspoons fresh chopped chives
¼ teaspoon salt
¼ teaspoon pepper
2 (2.1-ounce) packages frozen
    miniature phyllo shells, thawed
    (see note below)
6 bacon slices, cooked and crumbled

1 Drain and flake crabmeat, removing any bits of shell.

2 Combine crabmeat, sour cream, and next 4 ingredients, stirring well. Cover and chill. To serve, spoon crabmeat mixture into phyllo shells. Top with crumbled bacon. Serve immediately.

"You can find frozen miniature phyllo shells at your local supermarket. Once they're filled with this creamy crabmeat mixture and topped with bacon, you'll have an impressive appetizer that'll have your guests saying, 'OOH IT'S SO GOOD!!'"

Pepped-Up Oysters

1 dozen

12	oysters on the half shell
1	tablespoon vegetable oil
3	green onions, chopped
½	cup soft breadcrumbs (homemade) (see tip on page 92)
¼	cup grated Parmesan cheese
½	teaspoon black pepper
¼	teaspoon ground red pepper

1 Preheat the oven to Broil. Place oysters on a baking sheet; set aside.

2 Heat oil in a small skillet over medium-high heat. Sauté green onions in hot oil until tender. Add breadcrumbs, Parmesan cheese, black pepper, and red pepper, stirring well. Spoon breadcrumb mixture over oysters. Broil 5½" from heat 2 minutes or until golden. Serve immediately.

Aw, Shucks!

To shuck or open an oyster, hold the oyster, flat side up, firmly against a cutting board. Insert an oyster knife tip between the shells near the hinge. Twist the blade, and push it into the opening, prying the oyster open. Move the blade along the inside of the upper shell to free the muscle. Discard the top shell of the oyster and any bits of shell. Voila! You've got oysters on the half shell.

Chilie-Chicken Quesadillas

2 dozen appetizers

1¼ cups salsa, divided
1 cup chopped cooked chicken breast
1 (4.5-ounce) can chopped green
 chilies, drained
2 tablespoons chopped fresh cilantro
1 teaspoon ground cumin

6 (7") flour tortillas
1½ cups (6 ounces) shredded Monterey
 Jack cheese with peppers

1 Combine ½ cup salsa, the chicken, and next 3 ingredients.

2 Place 1 tortilla in a lightly greased skillet over medium-high heat. Immediately spoon about ⅙ of salsa mixture onto tortilla. Sprinkle with ¼ cup cheese, and heat 1 minute. Fold in half; cook 30 seconds or until lightly browned. Turn; cook other side 30 seconds or until browned. Repeat with remaining tortillas. Cut each tortilla into 4 wedges. Top with remaining ¾ cup salsa.

Chick Trick

Slash your prep time for this appetizer by using frozen diced cooked chicken breast instead of cooking your own. This handy product comes in an 18-ounce package in the frozen food section of your supermarket. Just take out what you need for this recipe and seal the remaining frozen chicken in a freezer-safe zip-top plastic bag.

Chicken Dippers with Sweet-Hot Chutney

6 to 8 appetizer servings

2 skinned and boned chicken breast halves

¼ teaspoon garlic salt

12 precooked bacon slices (see tip below)

½ cup hot mango chutney

½ cup salsa

1 Preheat the oven to 450°. Cut each chicken breast into 12 cubes. Sprinkle with garlic salt.

2 Cut bacon slices in half crosswise. Wrap bacon around each chicken cube; secure with wooden toothpicks. Arrange on a lightly greased rack of a broiler pan.

3 Bake at 450° for 10 to 12 minutes or until bacon is crisp.

4 Process chutney and salsa in a blender or food processor until smooth, stopping to scrape down sides. Serve with chicken bites.

A Bit About Bacon

Talk about a great product—we used precooked bacon in this recipe. Find it near the lunch meats at your local supermarket. The precooked kind saves you a step and delivers the full flavor of regular bacon.

Fudgy Hot Cocoa

12 cups

10 cups milk
1 cup chocolate flavor syrup
⅔ cup cocoa
⅔ cup hot fudge topping
2 teaspoons vanilla extract
½ teaspoon almond extract

1 Cook all ingredients in a Dutch oven over medium-low heat, stirring occasionally, 10 minutes or until thoroughly heated. (Do not boil.)

Marshmallow Matters

Here's a tip on how to add a holiday touch to this rich hot cocoa:

For the winter holidays, sprinkle some sugar onto wax paper; place 24 large marshmallows 2" apart on paper. Sprinkle with additional sugar, and top with wax paper. Flatten marshmallows with a rolling pin. Remove top sheet of wax paper, and cut marshmallows with snowflake cutters. Serve in hot cocoa.

For Halloween, substitute spooky cutters for a ghostly garnish. The kids can have fun any time of the year!

Hot Molasses Cider

4 cups

1	quart apple cider
¼	cup light molasses
1	(2¼") cinnamon stick
6	whole cloves
2	lemon slices
2	tablespoons lemon juice

1 Bring first 5 ingredients to a boil in a medium saucepan. Reduce heat, and simmer 10 minutes. Remove cinnamon stick and cloves, using a slotted spoon; discard. Stir in lemon juice, and serve immediately.

" I love the comforting aroma of this spiced cider. It's perfect on a cold winter night. And the lemon slices add flavor and a bit of sunshine to this warming wintertime brew."

Cherry Limeade

4 cups

1 (6-ounce) jar maraschino cherries with stems

1 Drain cherries, reserving ⅓ cup juice. Set aside 8 cherries, reserving remaining cherries for another use.

1 (6-ounce) can frozen limeade concentrate, thawed and undiluted
1 cup water

2 Combine ⅓ cup cherry juice, the limeade concentrate, and 1 cup water in a pitcher. Cover and chill thoroughly.

2 cups lime-flavored or plain sparkling water, chilled
Lime slices (optional)

3 Just before serving, stir in sparkling water. Serve with cherries over crushed ice. Garnish with lime slices, if desired.

No Meltdown Worries Here!

Rather than serving this fruity beverage over crushed ice, try freezing a little extra sparkling water in ice cube trays. This'll help prevent regular ice from diluting your drink. Add a stemmed cherry to each cube for a colorful touch. You're guaranteed a quick cooldown either way you serve it!

Lime-Mint Tea

10 cups

8½ cups water, divided
1½ cups sugar
6   regular-size tea bags
2   cups loosely packed fresh mint
      leaves, chopped

1½ cups fresh lime juice

1 Bring 4 cups water and the sugar to a boil in a saucepan, stirring until sugar dissolves; add tea bags. Cover and steep 5 minutes; discard tea bags. Stir in chopped mint; let stand 15 minutes.

2 Combine lime juice and remaining 4½ cups water in a large pitcher. Pour tea through a strainer into pitcher, discarding mint. Stir tea; cover and chill. Serve over ice.

As if iced tea weren't refreshing enough, I've added a little fresh mint and lime juice to perk up my favorite summertime cooler. If tea becomes cloudy after it's chilled, just add a little boiling water—that clears it up like magic!

Chocoholics' Smoothie

4½ cups

2   cups chocolate ice cream, softened
2   bananas, sliced
½   cup milk
¼   cup chocolate flavor syrup

Garnish: shaved chocolate (optional)

1 Process first 4 ingredients in a blender.

2 Add ice to 4½-cup level; process until smooth, stopping to scrape down sides. Garnish, if desired; serve immediately.

" Attention chocolate lovers: Here's the perfect fix for your next craving. You'll get a triple dose with chocolate ice cream, chocolate syrup, and shaved chocolate on top!"

Cinnamon Candy Punch

24 cups

1 cup water
½ cup sugar
⅓ cup red cinnamon candies (such as Red Hots)

2 (46-ounce) cans unsweetened pineapple juice, chilled
1 (2-liter) bottle raspberry-flavored ginger ale, chilled

1 Combine first 3 ingredients in a small saucepan; bring to a boil. Reduce heat, and simmer, uncovered, 5 minutes or until candies melt, stirring occasionally. Cool completely.

2 Combine cinnamon mixture and juice in a large punch bowl; stir well. Add ginger ale, stirring gently. Serve immediately.

" Use the cinnamon candies found in the candy section of the supermarket. They melt much better than those found in the cake mix section. "

Creamy Sherbet Punch

20 cups

9 cups water
1 (12-ounce) can frozen lemonade
   concentrate, thawed and undiluted
1 (6-ounce) can frozen orange juice
   concentrate, thawed and undiluted

½ gallon orange sherbet, softened
½ gallon vanilla ice cream, softened

1 Combine first 3 ingredients in a punch bowl.

2 Add sherbet and ice cream, stirring until creamy.

66 *The flavor combination of orange and vanilla ice cream makes this creamy concoction so-o-o good!* 99

Fancy Schmancy Dinners

" *Wow the whole gang with these simple, yet sophisticated meals. They'll think you slaved away in the kitchen for hours!* **"**

Grilled Jerk Chicken

4 servings

4	bone-in chicken breast halves
2	tablespoons jerk seasoning
2	tablespoons fresh lime juice
1	tablespoon vegetable oil

1 Preheat the grill.

2 Rinse chicken with cold water; pat dry with paper towels. Loosen skin from chicken breast with fingers without detaching skin. Rub jerk seasoning under skin; place skin back into position. Combine lime juice and oil; brush evenly over both sides of chicken.

3 Spray cold grill rack with nonstick cooking spray; place over medium heat (300° to 350°). Place chicken on grill rack; grill, covered, 10 minutes on each side or until chicken is done.

" For a lighter recipe, remove the skin from the chicken breasts. Brush with the lime juice mixture, rub with jerk seasoning, and then grill 'em up! You'll love these spicy chicken breasts either way. "

Basil-Glazed Chicken

4 servings

4	skinned, boned chicken breast halves
1	teaspoon salt
¼	teaspoon freshly ground pepper
1	tablespoon olive oil
2	tablespoons balsamic vinegar
1	tablespoon honey
2	tablespoons chopped fresh basil

1 Sprinkle both sides of chicken with salt and pepper.

2 Heat oil in a large nonstick skillet over medium-high heat. Add chicken; cook 5 minutes or until lightly browned. Turn chicken, and cook 6 minutes or until done. Stir in vinegar, honey, and basil; cook 1 more minute, turning chicken to coat with glaze.

" You're really gonna love the tangy-sweet flavors of this easy but oh-so-elegant glazed chicken. "

Orange-Glazed Chicken Tenders

4 servings

2	tablespoons vegetable oil
1	pound chicken tenders (see note below)
2	tablespoons all-purpose flour
2	green onions, sliced
1	clove garlic, minced
¾	cup orange juice
2	tablespoons soy sauce

1 Heat oil in a large skillet over high heat until hot. While skillet heats, dredge chicken tenders in flour. Add chicken to hot skillet, and cook 4 minutes or until browned, turning once. Remove chicken from skillet.

2 Reduce heat to medium-high; add green onions and garlic; cook, stirring constantly, 30 seconds. Add orange juice and soy sauce to skillet; bring to a boil. Cook, stirring constantly, 2 minutes or until mixture thickens slightly.

3 Return chicken to skillet; simmer 2 minutes or until chicken is thoroughly heated. Transfer to a serving platter.

> *Chicken tenders are thin, tender strips of breast meat. They're a popular new chicken product 'cause they cook up so quickly. If you can't find chicken tenders, just cut a pound of boneless breast into 3 or 4 strips each and flatten 'em slightly with a meat mallet or rolling pin. Voila!*

Tuscan Chicken and Beans

4 servings

2 teaspoons chopped fresh rosemary
　 or dried rosemary
¼ teaspoon garlic powder
¼ teaspoon salt
¼ teaspoon freshly ground pepper
4 skinned, boned chicken breast
　 halves

2 tablespoons olive oil
1 cup chicken broth
1 (16-ounce) can navy beans, rinsed
　 and drained

Fresh rosemary sprigs (optional)

1 Combine rosemary, garlic powder, salt, and pepper. Sprinkle half of rosemary mixture over chicken.

2 Heat oil in a large nonstick skillet over medium-high heat. Add chicken; cook 5 minutes on each side or until browned. Add remaining rosemary mixture, broth, and beans. Bring to a boil. Cover; reduce heat, and simmer 10 minutes. Uncover and simmer 10 more minutes or until chicken is done.

3 Spoon bean mixture into 4 shallow serving bowls. Top each with a chicken breast. Garnish with fresh rosemary sprigs, if desired.

" This rustic Italian one-dish meal turns plain chicken into an upscale dinner in no time. You can serve garlic bread with the chicken and finish off the meal with a refreshing fruit sorbet. Ooh it's so easy! "

Stuffed Chicken Rolls

(pictured on facing page)

6 servings

6	(6-ounce) skinned, boned chicken breast halves
½	teaspoon garlic salt
¼	teaspoon black pepper
½	cup chopped roasted sweet red peppers
1	(3-ounce) package cream cheese, softened
¼	cup pesto
¾	cup crushed cornflakes cereal
3	tablespoons grated Parmesan cheese
½	teaspoon paprika

1 Place chicken between 2 sheets of heavy-duty plastic wrap; flatten to ¼" thickness, using a meat mallet or rolling pin. Sprinkle chicken with garlic salt and black pepper; set aside.

2 Preheat the oven to 400°. Stir together red pepper, cream cheese, and pesto. Spread cheese mixture evenly over chicken breasts. Roll up, jellyroll fashion; secure with wooden toothpicks.

3 Combine crushed cereal, Parmesan cheese, and paprika. Dredge chicken in cereal mixture. Place in a lightly greased 7" x 11" pan. Bake, uncovered, at 400° for 26 to 28 minutes; let stand 5 minutes. Remove wooden toothpicks, and slice each roll into 6 rounds.

Roll On!
To save time, you can make these impressive chicken rolls ahead. Prepare the chicken through Step 2 and then park them in the fridge until you're ready for dinner. Dredge the rolls in the crispy coating right before baking.

Spicy Shrimp Creole,
page 85

Chicken Burrito Bundles, page 69

Beef-Vegetable Kabobs

(pictured on facing page)

6 servings

1½ pounds beef tenderloin steaks or boneless top sirloin
¾ cup red wine vinaigrette, divided
12 medium-size fresh mushrooms
6 medium jalapeño peppers (see tip on page 10)
2 medium-size yellow squash, cut crosswise into ½" slices
1 medium-size red onion, cut into 12 wedges

¼ cup hot jalapeño jelly

1 Cut steak into 1½" pieces. Place steak in a heavy-duty zip-top plastic bag. Add ½ cup vinaigrette. Seal bag; shake until steak is coated. Marinate in refrigerator 30 minutes, turning bag once. Remove steak from marinade; discard marinade. Thread steak and vegetables alternately onto 6 (15") metal or wooden skewers (see tip below).

2 Preheat the grill. Combine remaining ¼ cup vinaigrette and the jelly in a small saucepan. Cook over low heat, stirring constantly, until jelly melts.

3 Grill kabobs, covered, over medium-high heat (350° to 400°) 6 minutes on each side or until steak reaches desired degree of doneness, basting often with jelly mixture.

Some Like It Hot ...

... and some don't! For timid taste buds, use 1 small green bell pepper cut into 1" pieces instead of 6 whole jalapeños. Serve with yellow rice for a colorful and filling dinner. If you use wooden skewers, remember to soak them in warm water for 10 to 15 minutes before threading the steak and veggies!

Asian Beef Stir-Fry

3 to 4 servings

1   pound boneless top sirloin
2   tablespoons peanut or vegetable oil
2   cloves garlic, minced

1   (16-ounce) package frozen broccoli
        stir-fry vegetables, thawed
¼   cup oyster sauce or teriyaki sauce
Warm cooked rice

1 Slice meat diagonally across grain into very thin strips. Pour oil around top of a preheated wok or large nonstick skillet, coating sides; heat at medium-high (375°) until hot. Add meat and garlic; stir-fry until browned.

2 Add broccoli stir-fry vegetables and oyster sauce to wok; stir-fry 5 minutes or until thoroughly heated. Serve over warm cooked rice.

❝ As you start this stir-fry, put on the water for quick-cooking rice. Supper's ready when the stir-fry sizzle simmers down!❞

Peppercorn Steak with Mushroom Sauce

2 servings

1   tablespoon cracked peppercorns
½   teaspoon salt
2   beef tenderloin steaks (1" thick)

2   tablespoons vegetable oil
1   (8-ounce) package sliced fresh
      mushrooms
2   green onions, sliced
¼   cup dry red wine or canned beef
      broth

1 Preheat the oven to Broil. Combine cracked peppercorns and salt. Sprinkle both sides of steaks evenly with peppercorn mixture.

2 Place steaks on a lightly greased rack of a broiler pan; broil 5½" from heat 5 to 6 minutes on each side or to desired degree of doneness.

3 While steaks broil, heat oil over medium-high heat, and sauté mushrooms and onions 5 minutes or until mushrooms are tender. Add wine; simmer 1 minute.

4 Place steaks on a serving platter; spoon mushroom mixture over steaks.

Pep It Up!

To get the most punch from your pepper, crack your own peppercorns for this recipe. Freshly cracked pepper is more pungent than the ground pepper in cans or jars.

Speedy Flank Steak Teriyaki

4 servings

1 (1-pound) flank steak (½" thick)
¼ cup honey
¼ cup soy sauce
1 teaspoon ground ginger
1 teaspoon sesame oil
1 clove garlic, minced
¼ teaspoon salt
¼ teaspoon ground pepper

1 Score steak diagonally across grain at ¾" intervals. Place flank steak in a large heavy-duty zip-top plastic bag. Combine honey and remaining 6 ingredients; stir well. Pour marinade over steak; seal bag securely. Turn bag to coat steak.

2 Preheat the grill. Remove steak from marinade, reserving marinade. Place marinade in a small saucepan; bring to a boil. Remove from heat, and set aside.

3 Grill steak, covered, over medium-high heat (350° to 400°) 5 to 6 minutes on each side or to desired degree of doneness, basting occasionally with boiled marinade. Slice steak diagonally across grain into ¼"-thick slices.

" No time to marinate? No problem! For this recipe, you just score the top of the steak and let it soak in a pungent marinade while you heat up the grill. The flavors ooze into the meat in no time!"

Slow-Cooker Lasagna

4 servings

1   pound ground chuck
1   teaspoon dried Italian seasoning
1   (28-ounce) jar chunky garden-style
      spaghetti sauce
⅓   cup water

8   lasagna noodles, uncooked
1   (4½-ounce) jar mushrooms,
      undrained

1   (15-ounce) container ricotta cheese
2   cups shredded part-skim mozzarella
      cheese

1 Cook beef and Italian seasoning in a large skillet over medium-high heat, stirring until beef crumbles and is no longer pink; drain. Combine spaghetti sauce and water in a small bowl.

2 Place 4 uncooked noodles in a lightly greased 6-quart slow cooker. Layer with half each of beef mixture, spaghetti sauce mixture, and mushrooms.

3 Spread ricotta cheese over mushrooms. Sprinkle with 1 cup mozzarella cheese. Layer with remaining noodles, meat, sauce mixture, mushrooms, and mozzarella cheese. Cover and cook on HIGH setting 1 hour; reduce heat, and cook on LOW setting 5 hours.

Now That's Using Your Noodle!
You may never go back to regular lasagna again once you try this easy slow-cooker version where you don't even have to cook the noodles!

Grilled Lemon-Herb Veal Chops

4 servings

3	tablespoons fresh lemon juice
3	tablespoons olive oil
3	cloves garlic, quartered
2	teaspoons dried oregano
1	teaspoon freshly ground pepper
4	(1"-thick) veal loin chops

4 (¼") slices firm ripe tomatoes

1 Process first 5 ingredients in a food processor or blender until well blended, making a marinade. Reserve 1 tablespoon marinade. Coat both sides of chops with remaining marinade, and place in a shallow dish. Cover and marinate in refrigerator 2 hours.

2 Preheat the grill. Spread reserved 1 tablespoon marinade over 1 side of each tomato slice.

3 Grill chops, uncovered, over medium-high heat (350° to 400°) 12 to 14 minutes, turning once. Cover and grill 10 to 12 more minutes, turning once. Place tomato slices on grill during last 6 minutes of grilling time, turning once. Serve tomatoes alongside veal chops.

❝ Talk about fancy schmancy! Lemon, garlic, and oregano elevate mild veal chops to flavor perfection. When buying veal chops, look for meat that's pale pink to get the best quality. ❞

Grilled Lamb Chops

2 to 4 servings

¼   cup balsamic vinegar
1   tablespoon chopped fresh rosemary
        or dried rosemary
¼   teaspoon garlic powder
¼   teaspoon pepper
Salt
4   lamb loin chops (1" thick)

1 Preheat the grill. Stir together first 4 ingredients in a small bowl. Sprinkle salt on both sides of chops.

2 Grill chops, covered, over medium-high heat (350° to 400°) 7 minutes on each side or to desired degree of doneness, basting occasionally with vinegar mixture.

" If you have time, marinate the chops an hour or two in the refrigerator, and the chops will be even more flavorful. Serve with couscous, which is a boon to cooks because it cooks in 5 minutes flat! What a time-saver! "

Bourbon-Glazed Ham Steak

4 servings

¼ cup bourbon
3 tablespoons light brown sugar
3 tablespoons apple juice concentrate,
    undiluted
½ teaspoon stone-ground mustard

1 (½"-thick) ham slice (about
    1 ¼ pounds)
1 teaspoon vegetable oil

1 Combine first 4 ingredients; stir well.

2 Cook ham slice in hot oil in a large skillet over medium-high heat 2 minutes on each side or until lightly browned. Reduce heat to medium-low, and add bourbon mixture. Cook 9 minutes or until bourbon sauce is slightly thick, stirring sauce and turning ham occasionally. Cut slice into serving-sized pieces. Place slices on individual plates, and top with bourbon sauce.

❝Need a special entrée for last-minute company? Bourbon, apple juice, and mustard make a delectable glaze for ham steaks, and no one'll know you whipped up this dish in under 30 minutes. Serve green beans and puréed sweet potatoes with this to round out the meal.❞

Sesame Pork Kabobs

4 servings

1   pound boneless pork loin, sliced

3   tablespoons soy sauce
2   tablespoons sesame oil
2   tablespoons honey
1   teaspoon minced garlic
½   teaspoon hot sauce
1   teaspoon sesame seeds, toasted

1 Preheat the grill. Thread pork loin slices evenly onto 8 (6") metal or wooden skewers (see tip on page 41).

2 Stir together soy sauce and remaining 5 ingredients in a shallow dish; add pork kabobs. Cover and marinate in refrigerator 5 to 10 minutes while the grill heats.

3 Grill kabobs, covered, over medium-high heat (350° to 400°) 3 to 4 minutes on each side.

Veggie Variety

Throw some vegetables on the grill to pair with these flavorful kabobs. Select whatever's in season. Red, yellow, and green bell peppers, eggplant, zucchini, yellow squash, tomatoes, and onions all grill up nicely in no time. Brush the vegetables with olive oil, and sprinkle with salt and pepper before grilling.

Balsamic Pork Chops

4 servings

4   (¾"-thick) boneless center-cut loin
      pork chops
2   teaspoons lemon pepper
1   tablespoon vegetable oil

½   cup balsamic vinegar
⅓   cup canned chicken broth

1 Sprinkle chops evenly with lemon pepper. Heat oil in a heavy skillet over medium-high heat until hot; add chops. Cook 3 minutes on each side or until browned. Remove chops from skillet; keep warm.

2 Combine vinegar and broth in skillet, stirring to loosen any browned bits from pan. Cook over medium-high heat 4 minutes or until mixture is reduced to a thin sauce. Spoon over chops.

" Usually when you brown meat in a skillet, little caramelized bits of the meat will cling to the pan. These little nuggets are full of flavor, so 'deglaze' the skillet like the fancy chefs do. Add a little liquid to the skillet and stir the bits into a tasty sauce, like in this recipe. "

Pork Tenderloin with Black Bean Salsa

4 servings

½ cup fresh lime juice
½ teaspoon ground red pepper
½ teaspoon ground cumin
¼ teaspoon salt
4 cloves garlic, crushed
2 (¾-pound) pork tenderloins

1 (15-ounce) can black beans, rinsed
    and drained
1 cup salsa

1 Combine first 5 ingredients in a large heavy-duty zip-top plastic bag. Add pork; marinate in refrigerator 20 minutes.

2 Meanwhile, combine black beans and salsa, stirring well. Set aside.

3 Preheat the grill. Remove pork from bag, reserving marinade. Place marinade in a small saucepan; bring to a boil. Remove from heat, and set aside.

4 Spray cold grill rack with nonstick cooking spray, and place over medium-high heat (350° to 400°). Place tenderloins on rack. Grill, covered, 8 to 10 minutes on each side or until meat thermometer inserted into thickest part registers 160°, turning and basting with reserved marinade. Cut pork into thin slices, and serve with black bean salsa.

> " This simple pork dish will impress your guests without a lot of fuss. After you've grilled the tenderloins, let 'em stand for 5 to 10 minutes before slicing. These few minutes of resting time will ensure the pork will be juicy. "

Pork Medallions with Spinach

4 servings

1   (1½-pound) package lemon
     pepper-flavored pork tenderloin
     (see note below)

1   tablespoon vegetable oil
1   (10-ounce) package fresh spinach
4   green onions, thinly sliced
3   tablespoons fresh lemon juice
¼   teaspoon crushed red pepper
¼   teaspoon salt
¼   teaspoon black pepper

1 Trim fat from pork; slice tenderloin crosswise into ¾"-thick pieces. Place slices between 2 sheets of heavy-duty plastic wrap, and flatten to ¼" thickness, using a meat mallet or rolling pin.

2 Coat a large nonstick skillet with nonstick cooking spray; place over medium-high heat until hot. Add pork; cook 3 to 4 minutes on each side. Remove pork, reserving drippings in skillet. Set pork aside, and keep warm.

3 Heat oil in same skillet; add spinach and green onions. Cook, stirring constantly, 3 minutes or until spinach is just wilted. Add lemon juice and remaining 3 ingredients; toss well. Arrange spinach on plates. Top with pork slices. Serve immediately.

" Pork tenderloin comes packaged in a variety of flavors. We used the lemon pepper variety here, but feel free to substitute other flavors. If you use a peppercorn-flavored tenderloin, you may want to leave the black pepper out of the recipe but be sure to keep the crushed red pepper. It packs a powerful punch that's distinctive from black pepper. "

Blackened Catfish

4 servings

2 tablespoons paprika
2½ teaspoons salt
2 teaspoons lemon pepper
1½ teaspoons garlic powder
1½ teaspoons dried basil, crushed
1½ teaspoons ground red pepper
1 teaspoon onion powder
1 teaspoon dried thyme

4 catfish fillets (about 1½ pounds)
¾ cup unsalted butter, melted

1 Heat a large cast-iron or heavy aluminum skillet over medium-high heat 10 minutes.

2 Meanwhile, combine paprika and next 7 ingredients in a large shallow dish.

3 Dip fillets in butter, and dredge in seasoning mixture. Place on wax paper. Cook fillets, 2 at a time, 2 to 3 minutes on each side or until fish is blackened and flakes with a fork. Serve with lemon wedges.

" My secret seasoning blend works with any kind of fish. The trick is getting the pan hot enough before adding the fish. When a drop of water dances on the skillet, it's ready! "

Grecian Grouper

4 servings

4	(6-ounce) grouper fillets
1	tablespoon Greek seasoning
2	tablespoons butter
1	(10-ounce) package frozen chopped spinach, thawed and squeezed dry
1	plum tomato, coarsely chopped
¼	cup crumbled basil- and tomato-flavored feta cheese

1 Sprinkle both sides of fillets with seasoning. Melt butter in a large skillet over medium heat. Add fish, and cook 3 minutes; remove skillet from heat.

2 Turn fish; top with spinach, tomato, and cheese. Return skillet to heat; cover and cook 3 minutes or until spinach is hot and fish flakes with a fork.

For your family or for company, this Mediterranean-inspired grouper is perfect—and ready in under 15 minutes. Feta cheese, plum tomatoes, and Greek seasoning—a blend of oregano, garlic, black pepper, onion, and parsley—crown this fish with unbelievable flavor.

Grilled Honey-Mustard Salmon Steaks

2 servings

3 tablespoons honey mustard
1 tablespoon balsamic vinegar
¼ teaspoon coarsely ground pepper
½ teaspoon garlic salt
2 salmon steaks (¾" thick)

1 Preheat the grill. Combine first 4 ingredients in a bowl; brush mixture over salmon.

2 Grill salmon, covered, over medium-high heat (350° to 400°) 3 to 4 minutes on each side or until fish flakes with a fork. Serve immediately.

Aged to Perfection

Balsamic vinegar is a popular ingredient for marinades, sauces, and dressings. It's dark brown with a pungent sweetness that comes from aging in wood over a long period of time. It imparts a deep flavor in a variety of foods. You can find balsamic vinegar at the supermarket, or splurge on a bottle from a specialty store. If you don't have any on hand, you can substitute red wine vinegar, although it's a little tangier.

Shortcut Paella

6 servings

1   tablespoon vegetable oil
1   (16-ounce) package smoked
      sausage, sliced

1   pound unpeeled, medium-sized
      fresh shrimp (about 35 per pound)

2½   cups chicken broth
1   cup converted rice, uncooked
1   tablespoon curry powder
¼   teaspoon salt
1   (4-ounce) jar diced pimiento,
      undrained
1   (9-ounce) package frozen green
      peas

1 Heat oil in a large deep skillet over medium-high heat, and sauté sausage 10 minutes. Remove sausage, leaving drippings in skillet.

2 Peel shrimp, and devein, if desired; set aside.

3 Add broth to drippings in skillet, stirring to loosen particles from bottom of skillet; bring to a boil. Stir in rice, curry powder, and salt. Cover, reduce heat, and simmer 15 minutes. Stir in sausage, shrimp, and pimiento; cook 10 to 12 more minutes or until shrimp and rice are done. Stir in peas; cover and cook 1 to 2 more minutes.

" Paella, a traditional Spanish dish, may have different combinations of meat, seafood, and vegetables, but always has flavored rice. I like to use converted rice (the parboiled kind) in this recipe because it doesn't get gummy. "

One-Dish Cajun Shrimp Delish

6 servings

½ cup butter
¼ cup dry white wine
1 tablespoon Cajun seasoning
2 pounds unpeeled, large fresh
   shrimp (about 25 per pound)

1 Preheat the oven to 400°. Place butter in an ungreased 9" x 13" baking dish; place in oven until butter melts, about 4 minutes.

2 Stir wine, Cajun seasoning, and shrimp into butter in dish. Bake, uncovered, at 400° for 15 minutes or until shrimp turn pink, stirring occasionally. Serve in shallow bowls.

"Cajun seasoning is all the seasoning you need, especially in this 4-ingredient-favorite. Well, you do need one other thing—French bread for sopping up the spicy juices!"

Linguine and Mussels Marinara

3 to 4 servings

8   ounces linguine, uncooked

1   pound fresh, farm-raised mussels
2   cups chunky-style pasta sauce
¼   teaspoon crushed red pepper

¼   cup chopped fresh basil

1 Cook pasta according to package directions.

2 While pasta cooks, rinse mussels in cold water; remove beards on mussels, and scrub shells thoroughly with a brush. Discard any opened or cracked mussels. Combine mussels, pasta sauce, and red pepper in a large deep skillet. Cover and bring to a simmer over medium heat; cook 5 minutes or until mussels open. (Discard any unopened mussels.)

3 Place drained pasta into individual shallow bowls. Top with mussels and sauce; sprinkle with chopped basil. Serve immediately.

Mussel Know-How

Before preparing, tap mussels that have an opened shell. If they close, they're fine to cook; if they remain open, discard them along with any cracked mussels. To debeard a mussel, grasp the hairlike beard with your thumb and forefinger, and pull it away from the shell. Then the mussels are ready for a quick simmer.

Cheesy Ziti Toss

(pictured on page 2)

4 servings

8 ounces ziti pasta, uncooked

1 (15-ounce) can pasta-style
   tomatoes, undrained
1 ½ cups shredded Cheddar-mozzarella
   cheese blend
½ cup oil-packed dried tomatoes,
   drained and chopped
⅓ cup chopped kalamata olives
½ cup chopped red bell pepper
⅓ cup chopped fresh basil
½ teaspoon black pepper

1 Cook pasta according to package
directions.

2 While pasta cooks, stir together
tomatoes and remaining 6 ingredients in a large bowl. Drain pasta, and
combine immediately with tomato mixture; toss gently.

Tossing hot pasta with sauce ingredients that are room temperature warms the sauce in this recipe. You can't get much easier than that!

Fettuccine with Blue Cheese Alfredo

4 servings

¾ cup crumbled blue cheese, divided
1 (10-ounce) container refrigerated
   Alfredo sauce

2 ounces fresh spinach leaves

1 (9-ounce) package refrigerated
   fettuccine
3 ounces thinly sliced ham, cut into
   thin strips
2 tablespoons chopped fresh parsley
¼ cup pine nuts, toasted (see note
   below)

1 Combine ½ cup blue cheese and the
Alfredo sauce; set aside.

2 Stack several spinach leaves, and roll
stack, jellyroll fashion; cut roll into ¼"
slices to make thin spinach shreds.
Repeat with remaining spinach; set
aside.

3 Cook pasta according to package
directions. Drain pasta, and immediately toss with blue cheese Alfredo
sauce, spinach, ham, and parsley.
Sprinkle pasta with remaining ¼ cup
blue cheese and the pine nuts. Serve
immediately.

*Toasting nuts really brings out their flavor. You can toast this
small amount of pine nuts in a dry skillet over medium heat for
just a few minutes, stirring often. You can also substitute walnuts
for the pine nuts, if you'd like.*

Easy Weeknight Suppers

You'll have dinner on the table in no time flat with these quick-and-easy family pleasers!

Pepper-Jack Chicken

6 servings

¼ cup mayonnaise, divided
¾ cup (3 ounces) shredded Monterey
    Jack cheese with peppers
2 tablespoons chopped fresh cilantro
3 tablespoons sour cream
1 tablespoon finely chopped pickled
    jalapeño peppers
1 clove garlic, minced

6 skinned and boned chicken breast
    halves

1 Preheat the oven to Broil. Combine 3 tablespoons mayonnaise, the cheese, and next 4 ingredients, stirring well. Set aside.

2 Place chicken between 2 sheets of heavy-duty plastic wrap, and flatten to ¼" thickness, using a meat mallet or rolling pin. Brush both sides of chicken lightly with the remaining 1 tablespoon mayonnaise; place chicken on lightly greased rack in a broiler pan.

3 Broil 5½" from heat 5 minutes on each side. Spread cheese mixture evenly over chicken; broil 5 more minutes or until mixture is browned.

You can have this cheesy chicken dish ready in a flash. Pounding the chicken to an even thickness and then broiling it makes the chicken cook really fast. And I'm all for that!

Crunchy Lemon Chicken

4 servings

4	skinned and boned chicken breast halves
1	large egg, lightly beaten
¼	teaspoon salt
⅛	teaspoon ground red pepper
½	cup toasted wheat germ
2	tablespoons butter
3	tablespoons lemon juice

1 Place chicken between 2 sheets of heavy-duty plastic wrap, and flatten to ½" thickness, using a meat mallet or rolling pin.

2 Combine egg, salt, and pepper. Dip each piece of chicken in egg mixture, and dredge in wheat germ.

3 Melt butter in a large nonstick skillet over medium heat. Add chicken; cook 3 minutes on each side or until done. Remove chicken, and keep warm. Add lemon juice to skillet. Cook over high heat, deglazing skillet by scraping bits that cling to bottom; pour over chicken. Garnish with lemon slices, if desired.

Bunch of Crunch

Wheat germ adds nutty flavor and crunch to this dinnertime favorite. It also packs a nutritious dose of vitamins, minerals, and protein. Feel free to use fine, dry breadcrumbs from a can to coat the chicken, if you don't have wheat germ on hand.

Moroccan Chicken

4 servings

1 tablespoon olive oil

1 pound skinned and boned chicken breast halves, cut into 1" pieces

3 cups salsa

½ cup raisins

¼ cup sliced ripe or green olives

4½ teaspoons sugar

1½ teaspoons cinnamon

1 (5-ounce) package yellow rice mix

¼ cup pine nuts or slivered almonds, toasted

1 Heat olive oil in a Dutch oven over medium-high heat, and cook chicken 5 minutes or until done. Stir in salsa and next 4 ingredients. Reduce heat to low, and simmer, uncovered, 15 minutes.

2 Meanwhile, cook rice according to package directions. Serve chicken mixture over warm cooked yellow rice, and sprinkle each serving with nuts.

" The rich combination of raisins, olives, and cinnamon gives this dish a Moroccan accent. Toasted pine nuts or almonds finish it off with a nice crunch. "

Cheesy Chicken Penne

4 to 6 servings

8   ounces uncooked penne pasta

1   (16-ounce) loaf pasteurized
      prepared cheese product, cubed
1   (8-ounce) container sour cream
½   cup milk
2½ cups chopped cooked chicken

1 Cook pasta in salted water according to package directions; drain.

2 Cook cubed cheese, sour cream, and milk over medium-low heat 5 minutes or until cheese melts, stirring constantly. Stir in pasta and chicken, and cook until thoroughly heated.

> **"** If you want to spice things up, use 2 (8-ounce) loaves of pasteurized prepared cheese product with peppers instead of the plain version. The pepper variety adds a little extra kick, but you'll enjoy this quick pasta meal either way. **"**

Green Chilie-Chicken Lasagna

6 servings

2   (10-ounce) cans diced tomatoes
      and green chilies
1   (10¾-ounce) can cream of
      mushroom soup, undiluted
2   cups chopped cooked chicken
6   green onions, sliced

6   (7") flour tortillas
¼   cup chopped fresh cilantro
1   (8-ounce) package Monterey Jack
      cheese with peppers

1 Preheat the oven to 350°. Stir together diced tomatoes and green chilies and mushroom soup in a saucepan until blended. Cook over medium-high heat 6 to 8 minutes. Stir in chicken and green onions.

2 Arrange 2 tortillas in a lightly greased 7" x 11" baking dish, and spread one-third of tomato mixture on top; sprinkle with one-third of cilantro and one-third of cheese. Repeat layers twice, ending with cheese.

3 Bake at 350° for 30 minutes. Let stand 10 minutes before serving.

" Talk about quick— one-dish dinners like this Mexican lasagna are great for the busy cook. You'll be in and out of the kitchen in no time with this fast and fabulous family meal—with little cleanup! "

Chicken Parmesan Pizza

2 to 4 servings

1 (8-ounce) loaf garlic bread
4 large chicken fingers

½ cup marinara sauce

1 cup (4 ounces) shredded Italian
   cheese blend
2 tablespoons chopped fresh basil
   (optional)

1 Preheat the oven to 425°. Place garlic bread, butter side up, on a baking sheet. Arrange chicken fingers on the same baking sheet.

2 Bake at 425° for 10 minutes or until bread is lightly browned. Spread marinara sauce over garlic bread.

3 Cut chicken fingers into ½" strips, and arrange over marinara sauce. Sprinkle with cheese and, if desired, basil.

4 Bake at 425° for 5 to 10 minutes or until cheese melts.

Deli Delish

Take advantage of your supermarket's deli when you need a quick meal. Here we've combined deli chicken fingers and prepared garlic bread for a one-of-a-kind pizza. The kids will come running to the dinner table when they see not 1, but 2 all-time favorites—chicken fingers and pizza—brought together in this cheesy showstopper.

Poppy Seed Chicken Casserole

4 servings

3 cups chopped cooked chicken

1 (10¾-ounce) can cream of chicken soup, undiluted

1 (8-ounce) carton sour cream

1 tablespoon poppy seeds

1½ cups crushed round buttery crackers (40 crackers)

¼ cup butter, melted

1 Preheat the oven to 350°. Combine first 4 ingredients; spoon into a lightly greased 7" x 11" baking dish.

2 Combine crushed crackers and butter, and sprinkle over chicken mixture. Bake, uncovered, at 350° for 30 minutes.

Here's one of my all-time favorite casseroles! It's as simple as can be, but it's oh-so fancy tasting. Serve it with a tossed salad, and you've got dinner in a flash!

Chicken Burrito Bundles

(pictured on page 39)
6 servings

2	cups chopped cooked chicken
1	(1¼-ounce) package taco seasoning mix
1	(16-ounce) can refried beans
6	(8") flour tortillas
1	(8-ounce) package shredded sharp Cheddar cheese
3	plum tomatoes, diced
1	small onion, diced

1 Preheat the oven to 350°. Place chicken and seasoning mix in a large heavy-duty zip-top plastic bag; seal bag, and shake to coat.

2 Spread beans down center of tortillas. Top with chicken, cheese, tomatoes, and onion; roll up. Wrap each in aluminum foil.

3 Bake at 350° for 15 minutes. Serve with salsa.

Salsa

Bundle Up!
For a change, try serving these cheesy-chicken burritos with salsa verde, or green salsa, that's made from tomatillos and green chilies. You'll find it at the supermarket next to the traditional salsa.

Mongolian Beef

4 servings

2	tablespoons cornstarch
2	tablespoons dark sesame oil
2	tablespoons hoisin sauce (see note below)
¼	cup light soy sauce
1	(14½-ounce) can chicken broth
3	tablespoons vegetable oil, divided
2	pounds boneless top sirloin, cut into thin slices
2	bunches green onions, cut diagonally into 1½" slices

Warm cooked rice

1 Stir together first 5 ingredients until mixture is smooth.

2 Heat 1½ tablespoons vegetable oil in a large skillet or wok over medium-high heat 2 minutes. Add beef, in batches, and stir-fry 8 minutes or until no longer pink. Remove from skillet.

3 Pour remaining 1½ tablespoons vegetable oil in skillet; heat 2 minutes. Add the green onions, and stir-fry 5 minutes or until tender.

4 Add beef and cornstarch mixture to skillet, stirring constantly 1 minute or until mixture is thickened. Serve immediately over warm cooked rice.

"Don't let the hoisin sauce in this simple stir-fry scare you. You can find it at your local supermarket in the Asian food section. It's a sweet and spicy sauce that adds big flavor to the dish and will keep in the fridge for the next time you need it."

Swiss Steak Monterey

6 to 8 servings

⅓ cup all-purpose flour
½ teaspoon garlic salt
¼ teaspoon pepper
2 pounds cubed round or sirloin steak

3 tablespoons vegetable oil
2 (8-ounce) cans tomato sauce
1 (1.3-ounce) package dry onion
  soup mix

1 (8-ounce) container sour cream

1 Combine first 3 ingredients. Dredge cubed steak in flour mixture.

2 Heat oil in a Dutch oven over medium-high heat; add steak, in batches, and cook until no longer pink. Return all steak to pot. Stir in tomato sauce and soup mix; bring to a boil. Cover, reduce heat, and simmer 15 minutes. Remove steak to serving platter, reserving liquid in pot; keep warm.

3 Stir sour cream into tomato mixture; simmer, stirring constantly, until heated. (Do not boil.) Serve over steak.

Soup Mix Secret

We all know that dry soup mix is good for more than a bowl of onion soup. It's long been a staple at picnics and other get-togethers combined with sour cream as a dip for crackers or chips. Now try adding it to a sauce to enhance its flavor without a lot of fuss, like we did here.

Southwestern Burgers

(pictured on cover)

6 servings

½   cup mayonnaise
2½   tablespoons chopped green chilies
        (about ½ [4.5-ounce] can)

2   pounds ground chuck
1   small onion
1   teaspoon salt
1   teaspoon black pepper
2   teaspoons taco seasoning mix or
        chili powder

6   (1-ounce) slices Monterey Jack
        cheese with peppers

6   large sesame seed buns
1   (6-ounce) carton avocado dip
Toppings: curly leaf lettuce, red onion
        slices, tomato slices

1 Stir together mayonnaise and green chilies; cover and chill.

2 Preheat the grill. Stir together ground chuck, diced onion, salt, black pepper, and taco seasoning mix; shape into 6 patties.

3 Grill patties, covered, over medium-high heat (350° to 400°) 7 to 8 minutes on each side or until beef is no longer pink. Top patties with cheese, and grill 1 more minute or until cheese melts.

4 Place buns on grill, cut side down. Grill 1 minute or until lightly toasted. Serve patties on buns with avocado dip, desired toppings, and green chilie mayonnaise.

No ho-hum burgers here! I've turned the basic backyard burger into a towering fiesta of flavors. Pepper Jack cheese, avocado dip, and green chilie mayonnaise are star attractions!

Barbecue Meat Loaf

3 to 4 servings

1	pound ground chuck
½	cup barbecue sauce, divided
¼	cup chopped onion
¼	cup Italian-seasoned dry breadcrumbs
1	large egg
¼	teaspoon salt
¼	teaspoon pepper

1 Preheat the oven to 375°. Combine meat, ¼ cup barbecue sauce, the onion, breadcrumbs, egg, salt, and pepper in a large bowl; stir well.

2 Shape mixture into a 5" x 7" loaf on a lightly greased rack in a roasting pan. Spread the remaining ¼ cup barbecue sauce over loaf. Bake at 375° for 25 minutes or to desired degree of doneness.

Classic Comfort

Can you get more comforting than meat loaf? This classic dish gets even better if you pair it with garlic mashed potatoes. While the meat loaf cooks, combine 2⅔ cups frozen mashed potatoes (half of a 22-ounce package), 1¼ cups milk, and ¼ teaspoon each of salt, pepper, and garlic powder in a microwave-safe 1½-quart baking dish. Cook the potatoes according to package microwave directions. You'll have enough to serve with the meat loaf, and the gang will be beggin' for more.

Deep-Dish Pizza Casserole

6 servings

1   pound ground round
1   (15-ounce) can chunky Italian-style
      tomato sauce

1   (10-ounce) can refrigerated pizza
      dough
6   (1-ounce) slices mozzarella cheese,
      divided

¼   cup grated Parmesan cheese

1 Preheat the oven to 425°. Cook meat in a medium-sized nonstick skillet over medium-high heat, stirring until meat crumbles and is no longer pink. Drain, if necessary, and return to skillet. Add tomato sauce, and cook until heated.

2 Meanwhile, unroll pizza dough, and press into bottom and halfway up sides of a lightly greased 9" x 13" baking dish. Line bottom of pizza crust with 3 slices mozzarella cheese. Top with meat mixture.

3 Bake, uncovered, at 425° for 12 minutes. Top with remaining 3 cheese slices, and sprinkle with Parmesan cheese. Bake 5 more minutes or until crust is browned and cheese melts. Cool 5 minutes before serving.

" You'll be amazed how tasty this pizza casserole turns out. Make sure and push the pizza crust up the sides of your baking dish so the delicious pizza filling will bubble up inside a crispy crust. Serve it with a big tossed salad, and you've got a winner! "

Easy Beefy Casserole

4 to 6 servings

1   pound ground chuck
¼   teaspoon salt

½   (16-ounce) package frozen mixed
      vegetables
1   (10¾-ounce) can cream of chicken
      soup, undiluted
1   cup (4 ounces) shredded Cheddar
      cheese
½   (32-ounce) package frozen
      seasoned potato nuggets

1 Preheat the oven to 400°. Cook meat and salt in a large nonstick skillet over medium heat, stirring until meat crumbles and is no longer pink; drain. Spoon meat into a lightly greased 2½-quart shallow baking dish.

2 Layer frozen vegetables, soup, and cheese over meat. Top with frozen potato nuggets.

3 Bake casserole, uncovered, at 400° for 30 minutes or until potatoes are golden.

Your kids won't hesitate to dig into this casserole when they see that chunky 'tater topping! You'll be coming back for seconds, too!

Taco Beef Pot Pie

6 servings

2   (8-ounce) cans refrigerated crescent
     rolls, divided

1½ pounds ground chuck
½   small onion, minced
2   cups (8 ounces) shredded Cheddar
     cheese
½   cup water
½   cup chili sauce
2   tablespoons taco seasoning
1   tablespoon Worcestershire sauce
½   teaspoon pepper

1 Preheat the oven to 375°. Unroll 1 can crescent rolls, and press into a lightly greased 9" x 13" pan. Bake at 375° for 10 minutes or until lightly browned.

2 Cook meat and onion in a large skillet, stirring until beef crumbles and is no longer pink. Drain. Stir in cheese and remaining 5 ingredients; spoon over crust.

3 Unroll remaining can of crescent rolls on a lightly floured surface, and shape into a rectangle, pressing perforations to seal; cut into 1" strips. Arrange strips in a lattice design over beef mixture.

4 Bake at 375° for 20 minutes or until golden. Let stand 10 minutes. Serve with sour cream and salsa, if desired.

"I love the way this casserole turns out. It has that down-home lattice crust without all the old-fashioned time and effort. Canned crescent rolls are the perfect dough to make the lattice design, and the cheesy meat filling bubbles up beneath the checkerboard crust for a real eye-catching, come-and-get-it meal."

Honey-Garlic Pork Tenderloin

4 servings

¾ cup lemon juice

¾ cup honey

⅓ cup soy sauce

3 tablespoons dry sherry or chicken broth

5 cloves garlic, pressed

2 (¾-pound) pork tenderloins

1 Stir together first 5 ingredients in a shallow dish or heavy-duty zip-top plastic bag; remove 1 cup mixture for basting, and set aside. Pierce pork several times with a fork, and place in bag in remaining mixture. Cover or seal, and chill 1 hour.

2 Preheat the grill. Remove pork, discarding marinade.

3 Grill pork, covered, over medium heat (300° to 350°) 11 to 13 minutes on each side or until a meat thermometer inserted into thickest portion registers 160°, basting with reserved honey mixture.

❝ These tenderloins pack a flavor wallop with a honey-garlic marinade and basting sauce. They just have to marinate for an hour and then it's on to the grill. Use a meat thermometer to help you gauge exactly when the meat's finished cooking. If you cook tenderloin too long, it can be dry, so get it to 160°, then pull it off the grill! ❞

Asian Pork 'n' Rice

4 servings

1	tablespoon vegetable oil
1	(1-pound) pork tenderloin, cut into chunks
½	cup diced onion

2	cups water
1½	cups uncooked instant rice
3	tablespoons soy sauce
½	teaspoon garlic salt
2	cups shredded iceberg lettuce

1 Heat oil in a large skillet over medium-high heat, and cook pork 4 minutes or until browned. Add onion; cook 3 minutes or until tender, stirring constantly.

2 Add water and next 3 ingredients; bring mixture to a boil. Remove from heat; cover and let stand 5 minutes. Stir in lettuce just before serving. Serve with additional soy sauce, if desired.

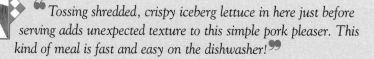

" Tossing shredded, crispy iceberg lettuce in here just before serving adds unexpected texture to this simple pork pleaser. This kind of meal is fast and easy on the dishwasher! "

Creamy Ham Casserole

4 servings

4   ounces medium egg noodles, uncooked

1   tablespoon vegetable oil
2   cups chopped cooked ham
1   medium-size green bell pepper, seeded and chopped
¼   cup chopped onion
¼   cup sliced celery
1   (10¾-ounce) can cream of mushroom soup, undiluted
1   (8-ounce) container sour cream

½   cup (2 ounces) shredded Cheddar cheese

1 Preheat the oven to 350°. Cook pasta according to package directions; drain.

2 Heat oil in a large skillet over medium-high heat, and cook ham and next 3 ingredients 5 minutes, stirring often. Remove from heat; stir in soup, sour cream, and pasta. Spoon into a lightly greased 1½-quart baking dish.

3 Cover and bake at 350° for 25 minutes. Sprinkle with cheese, and bake, uncovered, 5 more minutes. Let stand 10 minutes before serving.

Ham It Up!

Here's a great way to use leftover ham. Or, if you don't have any leftovers, take advantage of cubed cooked ham that's available in the meat counter of your supermarket. When you need just a few cups of ham, such as in this deliciously creamy recipe, that gives you an inexpensive head start for preparing a variety of meals.

Stromboli-in-a-Flash

5 servings

1   tablespoon vegetable oil
½   cup chopped onion

1   (10-ounce) can refrigerated pizza dough
2   tablespoons coarse-grained mustard
1   cup (4 ounces) shredded mozzarella cheese
6   ounces thinly sliced ham
1   teaspoon dried Italian seasoning

1   large egg, lightly beaten

1 Preheat the oven to 425°. Heat oil in a small skillet over medium-high heat, and sauté onion 4 minutes or until tender; set aside.

2 Unroll dough, and press into an 8" x 12" rectangle on a lightly greased baking sheet. Spread mustard over dough to within ½" of edges. Arrange cheese, onion, and ham lengthwise down center of dough, leaving a ½" border at both ends. Sprinkle seasoning over ham.

3 At 1" intervals on long sides of rectangle, cut slits from edge of filling to edge of dough. Alternating sides, fold strips at an angle across filling. Brush top of dough with egg. Bake at 425° for 12 to 14 minutes or until browned.

❝ I've made this rolled sandwich a little fancy without a lot of work. Cutting the pizza dough into strips on the edges and folding them over at an angle gives you a stromboli with a little extra class. If you're in a hurry, just fold the sides over the filling without cutting the strips. You'll have a yummy meal in minutes any way you slice it! ❞

Sausage, Peppers, and Mushrooms

5 servings

1 (1¼-pound) package Italian sausage links

1 cup dry white wine

1 medium onion, sliced

1 clove garlic, minced

2 medium-size green bell peppers, cut into strips

1 (8-ounce) package sliced fresh mushrooms

2 (8-ounce) cans tomato sauce

1 Brown sausage in a large heavy skillet; add wine. Bring to a boil; cover, reduce heat, and simmer 10 minutes or until sausage is no longer pink. Uncover, bring to a boil, and reduce wine by two-thirds. Remove sausage, reserving drippings in skillet; set sausage aside, and keep warm.

2 Add onion, garlic, green pepper, and mushrooms to skillet; sauté until tender. Return sausage to skillet; add tomato sauce. Simmer 10 minutes or to desired consistency.

66 This chunky blend of Italian sausage and veggies does double duty as a one-dish meal or as a sandwich filling spooned over French rolls. You're gonna love it 'cause it's easy and versatile! 99

Skillet Sausage 'n' Cabbage

4 servings

1   (16-ounce) package kielbasa sausage, cut into 1" pieces

1   medium onion, thinly sliced
1   green bell pepper, cut into strips
6   cups coarsely chopped cabbage
1   cup dry white wine or chicken broth
½   teaspoon caraway seeds
½   teaspoon salt
½   teaspoon black pepper

1 Sauté sausage in a large heavy skillet over medium heat until browned; drain on paper towels.

2 Add onion and bell pepper to skillet, and sauté 2 to 3 minutes. Add cabbage, and cook, stirring often, 8 minutes. Add sausage, wine, and remaining ingredients. Reduce heat to medium-low, and cook 10 minutes or until cabbage is tender. Serve immediately.

"What could be better on a cold winter night than a skillet supper bursting with the hearty flavors of smoked sausage and cabbage? Oh, it's so comforting!"

Baked Fish with Parmesan-Sour Cream Sauce

4 to 6 servings

1 ½ pounds orange roughy fillets
(see note below)

1 (8-ounce) container sour cream
¼ cup shredded Parmesan cheese
½ teaspoon paprika
½ teaspoon salt
¼ teaspoon pepper
2 tablespoons Italian-seasoned
breadcrumbs
2 tablespoons butter, melted

1 Preheat the oven to 350°. Place fillets in a single layer in a lightly greased 9" x 13" pan.

2 Stir together sour cream and next 4 ingredients; spread mixture evenly over fillets. Sprinkle with breadcrumbs, and drizzle with butter.

3 Bake at 350° for 20 to 25 minutes or until fish flakes with a fork.

" Tilapia, flounder, or any other white fish can work in place of orange roughy in this recipe. Whichever type you choose, I promise you, one bite and you're hooked! "

Grouper Fingers

3 servings

1 (1-pound) grouper
2 large eggs, lightly beaten
18 saltines, crushed

Canola oil
¼ teaspoon salt

1 Cut fish into 5" x 1½" strips. Dip in egg, and dredge in saltine cracker crumbs.

2 Pour oil to a depth of 1½" into a heavy skillet; heat oil to 375°. Fry fish, in batches, 2 minutes on each side. Drain on paper towels, and sprinkle with salt.

Saltine crackers make a dandy crunchy coating for these homemade fish sticks. Serve 'em with tartar sauce for dipping, and you'll have a dinnertime winner every time.

Spicy Shrimp Creole

(pictured on page 38)
4 servings

1 pound unpeeled, medium-size fresh shrimp (about 35 per pound)

2 tablespoons olive oil
1 small onion, chopped
1 small green bell pepper, chopped
½ teaspoon crushed red pepper
6 cloves garlic, minced
2 (14½-ounce) cans Cajun-style stewed tomatoes, undrained

1 Peel and devein shrimp; set aside.

2 Heat olive oil in a large skillet over medium-high heat; sauté onion and next 3 ingredients until tender. Add tomatoes. Bring to a boil; reduce heat, and simmer, uncovered, 10 minutes, stirring occasionally. Add shrimp.

3 Cover and cook 5 minutes or until shrimp turn pink. Serve over warm cooked rice.

Even Quicker?

Yup, there are ways to make this recipe even quicker. You can ask your grocer to peel and devein the shrimp for you. (You'll only need about ¾ pound of the already peeled shrimp, if it's sold that way.) Try using frozen onions and green bell peppers instead of chopping fresh ones. And last but not least, prepare quick-cooking rice to make your life even easier. You'll be amazed how quickly you can get this on the table!

Angel Hair Pasta with Clams

4 servings

8   ounces dried angel hair pasta, uncooked

1   tablespoon olive oil
1½ teaspoons minced garlic
3   (6½-ounce) cans minced clams

⅓   cup shredded Parmesan cheese
Freshly ground pepper

1 Cook pasta according to package directions.

2 While pasta cooks, heat oil in a large skillet over medium heat. Add garlic; sauté 2 minutes. Drain clams, reserving liquid. Add clam liquid to skillet, and simmer 5 minutes. Add clams; simmer 5 more minutes.

3 Combine drained pasta and clam mixture in a serving bowl; toss gently. Sprinkle with cheese and pepper. Serve immediately.

"You may be surprised at what you can create with canned clams. I know you'll love this to-die-for pasta dish that's ready in mere minutes. Steamed broccoli and French bread will round out the meal perfectly. So, what are you waiting for? Get cooking!"

Eggplant Parmesan

4 servings

1 (1½-pound) eggplant, peeled if desired (see tip below)
1 cup shredded Parmesan cheese
2 cups (8 ounces) shredded mozzarella cheese, divided
1½ cups spaghetti sauce or marinara sauce

1 Preheat the oven to 375°. Cut eggplant into ¼"-thick slices. Layer half of eggplant, half of Parmesan cheese, ¾ cup mozzarella, and half of spaghetti sauce in a lightly greased 7" x 11" baking dish. Repeat layers.

2 Cover and bake at 375° for 40 minutes or until eggplant is tender. Uncover, top with remaining ½ cup mozzarella cheese, and bake 5 more minutes or until cheese melts.

Eggplant 101

When buying eggplant, choose one that's firm, smooth-skinned, and heavy for its size. You should peel eggplant that's very ripe 'cause the skin may be tough, but the skin of young eggplant is tender and delicious. Serve Eggplant Parmesan as a meatless main dish or as a side dish.

Easy Chilies Rellenos

4 to 6 servings

2   (4.5-ounce) cans chopped green
    chilies, undrained
1   pound Monterey Jack cheese, cut
    into ½" cubes
1   (2¼-ounce) can sliced ripe olives,
    drained

4   large eggs, lightly beaten
½   cup milk
½   teaspoon dry mustard
¼   teaspoon salt

1 Preheat the oven to 325°. Layer one-third each of green chilies, cheese, and olives in a greased 7" x 11" baking dish. Repeat layers twice.

2 Combine eggs and remaining 3 ingredients in a medium bowl; pour over cheese mixture.

3 Bake, uncovered, at 325° for 35 minutes. Remove from oven, and let stand 5 minutes before serving. Cut into squares to serve.

Chilies Rellenos, pronounced CHEE-lehs rreh-YEH-nohs, translates to 'stuffed peppers' that are dipped in an egg batter and fried. We've made things simpler with this dish by layering chilies, cheese, and olives, and pouring an egg batter over the top. You get all the classic flavors of Chilies Rellenos without all the fuss. Now, how's that for a simply great—or great, simple—meal?!

Super Sideshow

"Complete your next meal with one of these super easy side dishes, and wait for the raves to roll in!"

Roasted Asparagus

4 servings

1   pound fresh asparagus

½   cup freshly grated Parmesan cheese
1   tablespoon grated lemon rind
½   teaspoon salt
½   teaspoon freshly ground pepper
2   tablespoons olive oil

1 Preheat the oven to 400°. Snap off tough ends of asparagus. Arrange asparagus in a single layer in a rimmed baking sheet.

2 Sprinkle with cheese, lemon rind, salt, and pepper. Drizzle with oil. Bake, uncovered, at 400° for 9 minutes or until tender.

" Roasting is one of my favorite ways to cook veggies 'cause the high temperature cooks 'em so quickly and caramelizes 'em for great flavor. You've got a gourmet side dish in less than 10 minutes! "

Home-Style Green Beans

3 servings

¾ pound fresh green beans, trimmed and cut into 2" pieces
1½ cups water

6 bacon slices, cooked and crumbled
1 teaspoon seasoned salt

1 Combine green beans and water in a medium saucepan; bring to a boil. Cover, reduce heat, and simmer 5 minutes or until crisp-tender.

2 Add bacon and seasoned salt; simmer 10 to 15 more minutes. Serve with a slotted spoon.

66 'Home-style' reflects the old-time flavor and tenderness of these green beans. They'll make everyone want to eat their veggies! 99

Best Broccoli Casserole

6 servings

2   (10-ounce) packages frozen
        chopped broccoli

1   (10¾-ounce) can cream of celery
        or cream of mushroom soup,
        undiluted
1   (8-ounce) can sliced water
        chestnuts, drained
1   (4-ounce) can sliced mushrooms,
        drained
¼   teaspoon seasoned salt
1   cup soft homemade breadcrumbs
        (see tip below)
1   cup (4 ounces) shredded sharp
        Cheddar cheese
1   tablespoon butter, melted

1 Preheat the oven to 350°. Cook broccoli according to package directions; drain.

2 Combine broccoli, soup, and next 3 ingredients. Spoon into a lightly greased 1½-quart baking dish. Combine breadcrumbs, cheese, and butter. Sprinkle crumb mixture over broccoli mixture. Bake, uncovered, at 350° for 30 minutes.

That's the Way It Crumbles

To make homemade breadcrumbs, process bread slices in a food processor or blender. It takes about 2 slices of bread to make 1 cup of soft breadcrumbs. Tossin' 'em with the butter and cheese makes a tasty home-style topping on this side-dish favorite.

Corn-Rice Casserole

10 to 12 servings

2 cups uncooked long-grain rice

2 tablespoons butter
1 green bell pepper, chopped
1 small onion, chopped

1 (15½-ounce) can cream-style corn
2 (11-ounce) cans Mexican-style corn, drained
1 (10-ounce) can diced tomato and green chilies, undrained
1 (8-ounce) loaf mild Mexican pasteurized prepared cheese product, cubed
½ cup (2 ounces) shredded Cheddar cheese

1 Preheat the oven to 350°. Cook rice according to package directions; set aside.

2 Melt butter in a large skillet over medium heat; add bell pepper and onion, and sauté 5 minutes or until tender.

3 Stir in cooked rice, cream-style corn, and next 3 ingredients; spoon into a lightly greased 9" x 13" baking dish.

4 Bake, uncovered, at 350° for 30 minutes or until thoroughly heated; top with shredded cheese, and bake 5 more minutes or until cheese melts.

A Favorite for Freezin'
Friends always call and ask for recipes they can prepare ahead and freeze. Well, this recipe works great for that! To freeze it, line the baking dish with aluminum foil; fill and freeze. Lift the frozen casserole from the dish, and wrap it tightly with foil; return to the freezer. When you're ready to cook it, remove the foil, and place frozen casserole back into the serving dish. Let it stand at room temperature for 30 minutes. Then bake it as directed above, and get ready for rave reviews!

Grilled Portobello "Steaks"

4 servings

4   large portobello mushrooms (about
        3 to 4 ounces each)
½   cup olive oil
2   cloves garlic, minced
1   teaspoon salt
2   teaspoons Worcestershire sauce
½   teaspoon freshly ground pepper

1 Clean mushrooms and cut stems off near the caps. Reserve stems for other uses. Place mushroom caps, gill side up, on a plate. Combine olive oil and remaining 4 ingredients. Spoon oil mixture evenly into gills of each mushroom. Cover and chill if not grilling immediately.

2 Preheat the grill. Place mushrooms, gill side up, on grill rack. Grill, covered, over medium heat (300° to 350°) 4 minutes. Turn mushrooms; grill, covered, 4 minutes or just until tender.

King of the Mushroom

These big chunky portobellos grill up almost like a steak! Slice 'em up with a knife and fork as a side dish or top 'em with provolone cheese and turn 'em into a "beefy" burger with or without the bun as a main dish. You can grill 'em immediately after you douse them in the oil mixture if you don't have time for chilling.

Honey-Orange Parsnips

3 to 4 servings

1	cup water
1	pound parsnips, sliced

3	tablespoons butter
1	tablespoon honey
1	teaspoon grated orange rind
1	tablespoon fresh orange juice

1 Bring water to a boil in a medium saucepan. Add parsnips; cover and cook 8 minutes or just until tender. Drain.

2 Return parsnips to pan; add butter and remaining ingredients, stirring gently until butter melts. Place pan over medium heat, and cook, uncovered, 1 to 2 minutes or until parsnips are glazed, stirring occasionally.

Partial to Parsnips

Honey and orange lend a sweet-tangy flavor to this slightly sweet vegetable that looks like a white carrot. Slice parsnips and prepare 'em just like carrots. In fact, if parsnips aren't available, you can use carrots in this recipe, if you'd like.

Easy Black-Eyed Peas

4 servings

½   (16-ounce) package kielbasa, sliced
     and drained

1   (16-ounce) package frozen
     black-eyed peas
3   cups water
2   large beef bouillon cubes
1   medium onion, chopped

1 Sauté kielbasa in a large skillet over medium-high heat until browned. Drain sausage, and return to skillet.

2 Add peas and remaining ingredients; bring to a boil. Reduce heat, and simmer 30 minutes or until tender.

66 *A little bit of sausage adds a lot of flavor to these peas. When fresh summer veggies start appearing at the supermarket or local farmer's stand, try this recipe with fresh black-eyed peas. You'll have to cook the shelled peas about 10 more minutes, but, boy, it's well worth the wait!* 99

Chili Fries

4 servings

1 tablespoon olive oil
2 teaspoons chili powder or Cajun
   seasoning
½ teaspoon salt
½ teaspoon dried oregano
¼ teaspoon garlic powder
¼ teaspoon ground cumin
3 medium baking potatoes (about 1½
   pounds), unpeeled

1 Preheat the oven to 450°. Combine first 6 ingredients in a large bowl. Peel potatoes, and cut into ¼"-thick strips. Add potato strips to olive oil mixture; toss gently to coat.

2 Arrange potato strips in a single layer on a baking sheet lightly coated with nonstick cooking spray. Bake, uncovered, at 450° for 25 minutes or until golden brown.

" Try leaving the peels on the potatoes to give these spicy fries a rustic appeal and an earthy flavor. Take your pick of chili powder or Cajun seasoning to jazz them up. Then sit back and watch them disappear! "

Garlic Mashed 'Taters

5 servings

4 medium baking potatoes (about 2½ pounds)

2 tablespoons butter
2 to 3 medium cloves garlic, minced
1¼ cups milk

¼ teaspoon salt
⅛ teaspoon pepper

1 Scrub potatoes, and pierce several times with a fork. Place potatoes, 1" apart, on a microwave-safe rack or paper towels. Microwave at HIGH 15 to 17 minutes or until potatoes are tender; let stand 5 minutes. Peel potatoes; mash and place in a microwave-safe dish.

2 Microwave butter and garlic in a 2-cup glass measuring cup at HIGH 30 seconds to 1 minute or until butter is melted; add milk, and microwave at HIGH 2 minutes.

3 Pour milk mixture into mashed potatoes, stirring to blend. Add salt and pepper. Microwave at HIGH 1 to 2 minutes or until thoroughly heated.

"Nothing makes me happier than using the microwave to speed things up at dinnertime. You'll never even touch the oven or cooktop when making these garlicky homemade 'taters."

Wilted Spinach

8 servings

2	pounds fresh spinach
3	bacon slices
2	medium onions, thinly sliced
½	cup chopped fresh parsley
2	tablespoons white wine vinegar
1	teaspoon chopped fresh rosemary (optional)
1	teaspoon salt
¼	teaspoon pepper

1 Remove stems from spinach. Wash leaves thoroughly, and pat dry with paper towels; tear into large pieces. Set aside.

2 Cook bacon in a large Dutch oven until crisp. Remove bacon; drain on paper towels, reserving 2 tablespoons drippings in Dutch oven. Crumble bacon, and set aside.

3 Sauté onion in hot drippings in pan over medium heat until tender. Add spinach, parsley, and remaining 4 ingredients; sauté 3 to 5 minutes or until spinach wilts and is tender. Top with crumbled bacon. Serve immediately.

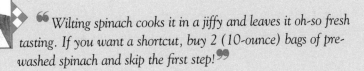

Wilting spinach cooks it in a jiffy and leaves it oh-so fresh tasting. If you want a shortcut, buy 2 (10-ounce) bags of pre-washed spinach and skip the first step!

Acorn Squash Toss

4 servings

1   acorn squash (about 1½ pounds)
      (see tip below)

2   tablespoons butter
1   clove garlic, minced
2   tablespoons soy sauce
¼   teaspoon salt
2   teaspoons sesame seeds, toasted

1 Cut squash in half, and remove seeds. Cut squash into 1" pieces.

2 Arrange squash in a steamer basket over boiling water. Cover and steam 10 to 12 minutes or to desired tenderness. Set aside.

3 Heat butter in a large skillet over medium-high heat until melted; add garlic. Cook, stirring constantly, until garlic begins to brown. Add squash, soy sauce, and salt, tossing gently. Sprinkle with sesame seeds. Serve immediately.

Skin Trick
Leaving the skin on the acorn squash not only adds to the flavor and fiber of this dish but also makes preparation a snap! The skin tenderizes as the squash cooks, and it's yummy eaten right along with the tender flesh.

Tempura Vegetables

4 servings

2	medium zucchini
2	medium-size yellow squash
1	medium onion

¾	cup cornstarch
½	cup self-rising cornmeal
¼	teaspoon pepper
½	cup water
1	large egg, lightly beaten

Corn oil

½   teaspoon salt

1 Cut zucchini, yellow squash, and onion into ¼"-thick slices. Separate onion slices into rings.

2 Combine cornstarch, cornmeal, and pepper; stir in ½ cup water and egg until smooth.

3 Pour oil to a depth of ½" into a heavy skillet; heat to 375°.

4 Dip vegetables into batter. Fry vegetables, in batches, 4 minutes or until golden. Drain on paper towels; sprinkle with salt.

Tempura is a fancy schmancy name for batter-dipped, deep-fried slices of vegetables. I like to serve 'em with soy sauce, zesty horseradish sauce, or sweet-and-sour dipping sauce. Try these for a change of pace—nothing plain or boring about 'em!

Grilled Pineapple

8 servings

1 medium-size fresh pineapple,
  peeled and cored
¼ cup teriyaki sauce
2 tablespoons brown sugar
2 teaspoons vegetable oil

1 Preheat the grill. Cut pineapple crosswise into 8 slices; place in a 9" x 13" baking dish. Combine teriyaki sauce, sugar, and oil, stirring well. Pour teriyaki mixture over pineapple, turning pineapple to coat. Let stand at room temperature 15 minutes, turning pineapple once. Remove pineapple from marinade; discard marinade.

2 Coat a cold grill rack with nonstick cooking spray; place on grill over medium-high heat (350° to 400°). Place pineapple on rack; grill, covered, 2 minutes on each side or until pineapple is tender.

" I like to buy fresh pineapple already peeled and cored to save even more time. You won't believe how the flavor of pineapple comes alive after a round on the grill. It's a juicy, sweet side dish that's sure to be a hit! It's a great accompaniment with pork or chicken. Stir up a purple cabbage slaw to serve alongside, and you've got a great-lookin', great-tastin' meal! "

Nutty Raisin Couscous

6 to 8 servings

1½ cups chicken broth
1½ cups water
½   cup raisins
2   tablespoons butter or olive oil
¼   teaspoon salt
¼   teaspoon pepper

1½ cups uncooked couscous
¼   cup pine nuts, toasted

1 Stir together first 6 ingredients in a saucepan; bring to a boil, stirring occasionally.

2 Stir in couscous; cover, remove from heat, and let stand 5 minutes or until liquid is absorbed. Fluff couscous with a fork, and sprinkle with pine nuts. Serve immediately.

When you're tired of plain old rice, shake things up with couscous. You'll find it's just what you need when you want a quick side. It cooks in 5 minutes, and the combination of raisins and pine nuts in this version will have 'em comin' back for more.

Quick-and-Easy Macaroni and Cheese

(pictured on facing page)

6 servings

8 ounces large elbow macaroni, cooked

1 (8-ounce) package shredded sharp Cheddar cheese

1 (10¾-ounce) can cream of mushroom soup, undiluted

½ cup mayonnaise

½ cup milk

½ cup soft, coarse breadcrumbs, made from French bread, lightly toasted (homemade) (see tip on page 92)

1 tablespoon butter, melted

1 Preheat the oven to 375°. Stir together first 5 ingredients in a lightly greased broilerproof 2-quart baking dish.

2 Bake at 375° for 22 to 25 minutes or until bubbly. Set the oven to Broil. Stir together breadcrumbs and butter; sprinkle over casserole. Broil 5½" from heat for 45 seconds to 1 minute or until lightly browned.

Lighten Up!

You can easily lighten this recipe by substituting a few ingredients: Use reduced-fat sharp Cheddar cheese, reduced-fat cream of mushroom soup, light mayonnaise, and fat-free milk for guilt-free mac 'n' cheese!

Italian Tomato-Corn Soup,
page 121

Basil Pesto Focaccia,
page 149

Vegetable-Wild Rice Medley

(pictured on facing page)

4 servings

1 tablespoon olive oil
1 cup chopped green bell pepper
¾ cup chopped onion
¾ cup finely chopped carrot
1 (8-ounce) package sliced fresh
   mushrooms

1 (2¾-ounce) package instant wild
   rice, uncooked
1⅓ cups chicken broth
¼ teaspoon black pepper

1 Heat oil in a saucepan over medium-high, and sauté next 4 ingredients until carrot is tender.

2 Add rice and broth. Bring to a boil; reduce heat, and simmer, uncovered, 5 minutes or until liquid is absorbed. Stir in black pepper. Let stand 5 minutes.

Sometimes I turn this veggie side dish into an easy entrée by stirring 1 cup of chopped cooked chicken into the rice after all the liquid's absorbed. It's a one-dish meal that's ready in a flash, and it's so delish!

Pork Fried Rice

4 servings

5   tablespoons soy sauce, divided
1   clove garlic, minced
¼   teaspoon sugar
¼   teaspoon dark sesame oil
¼   pound boneless pork loin chops, cut
      into thin strips

2   tablespoons canola oil
¾   pound fresh bean sprouts
3   cups cold cooked rice
1   cup sliced green onions

1 Stir together 2 tablespoons soy sauce, the garlic, sugar, and sesame oil in a bowl. Add pork, and toss well. Cover and chill 15 minutes.

2 Heat canola oil in a large nonstick skillet or wok over medium-high heat 1 to 2 minutes. Add pork mixture; stir-fry 2 minutes or until lightly browned. Add bean sprouts and rice, and stir-fry 2 minutes or until rice is thoroughly heated. Add green onions and remaining soy sauce; toss well. Serve immediately.

Fried Rice Trick

Want to know how to stir up fried rice that keeps its texture? Start with cold cooked rice. Just double-batch it the next time you cook plain rice for a side dish, and chill the leftovers. Then you can stir up this specialty in a jiffy.

Saffron Rice

6 servings

½ cup butter, melted
1 small onion, chopped
2 cups uncooked long-grain rice
¼ teaspoon ground saffron (see note below)

1 (32-ounce) container chicken broth
¼ teaspoon freshly ground pepper
½ cup raisins

1 Melt butter in a Dutch oven, and sauté onion 5 minutes. Stir in rice and saffron; sauté 5 minutes.

2 Add broth and pepper; bring to a boil. Cover, reduce heat, and simmer 20 minutes or until liquid is absorbed and rice is tender. Remove from heat, and stir in raisins. Cover and let stand 5 minutes.

You'll never want plain rice again when you stir up this colorful, flavorful version. Saffron tints it golden, broth flavors it just right, and raisins add a touch of sweetness. This dish accompanies chicken and pork dishes with real flair! Since saffron can be pricey, it's okay to substitute an equal amount of turmeric for it here.

Not-Too-Blue Cheese Grits

8 servings

4	cups water
2	cups chicken broth
1	teaspoon salt
1	teaspoon pepper
2	cups uncooked regular grits
¼	cup butter
8	ounces blue cheese, crumbled
6	ounces Baby Blue Saga cheese, crumbled

1 Combine first 4 ingredients in a saucepan; bring to a boil. Stir in grits and butter.

2 Cook grits according to package directions, stirring occasionally. Remove from heat; stir in cheeses. Serve warm with sliced tomatoes, if desired.

"These grits are a brunch and side-dish favorite at my house, even among those who don't consider themselves blue cheese fans. A combination of creamy Baby Blue Saga—a soft, mellow cheese, and the firmer regular blue cheese makes this too good to resist! If you can't find Baby Blue Saga, just use 14 ounces of regular blue cheese instead."

Soup and Salad Bar

"Fresh, homemade soups and salads are just a few steps away! Shh . . . it's our secret how easy they are!"

Pronto Gazpacho

4⅔ cups

10 green onions, sliced
2 small green bell peppers, diced
2 small cucumbers, diced
4 plum tomatoes, diced
2 cups Bloody Mary mix or vegetable
   juice
½ teaspoon salt
½ teaspoon black pepper

⅔ cup croutons

1 Stir together first 7 ingredients. Cover and chill at least 1 hour before serving.

2 Sprinkle each serving of soup with croutons.

Horsin' Around

You'll love the refreshing flavors of this chilled vegetable soup. For an extra garnish and a little kick that carries out the Bloody Mary theme, stir ½ teaspoon prepared horseradish into ⅓ cup sour cream, and dollop it on top with the croutons.

Blender Raspberry Soup

4⅔ cups

2 cups fresh or frozen raspberries, thawed
1 cup rosé or dry white wine
1 cup packed brown sugar
1 cup sour cream

1 Process all ingredients in a blender until smooth, stopping to scrape down sides.

2 Pour mixture through a wire-mesh strainer into serving bowls. Garnish with fresh raspberries or lime slices, if desired.

Pick-a-Berry Soup

The beauty of this quickie soup is that you can change up the berry to suit the season. Strawberries, blueberries, blackberries—they all taste great!

Tomato-Basil Bisque

7 cups

2   (10¾-ounce) cans tomato soup, undiluted
1   (14½-ounce) can diced tomatoes
2½ cups buttermilk
2   tablespoons chopped fresh basil
¼   teaspoon freshly ground pepper

1 Cook all ingredients in a 3-quart saucepan over medium heat 6 to 8 minutes or until mixture is thoroughly heated, stirring often. Serve immediately, or serve chilled.

"Canned tomato soup gets a flavor boost from buttermilk and fresh basil in this tasty little teaser. I've served it warm, and I've served it cold—either way it'll be a hit!"

Can-Can Bean Soup

10 cups

1   tablespoon vegetable oil
1   large onion, chopped
1   small green bell pepper, chopped

1   (16-ounce) can kidney beans, rinsed
       and drained
1   (15-ounce) can pinto beans, rinsed
       and drained
1   (15-ounce) can black beans, rinsed
       and drained
2   (14½-ounce) cans stewed tomatoes,
       undrained
1   (14-ounce) can chicken broth
1   cup picante sauce
1   teaspoon ground cumin

1 Heat oil in a large saucepan over medium-high heat, and sauté onion and bell pepper until tender.

2 Add kidney beans and remaining ingredients; bring to a boil. Cover, reduce heat, and simmer 10 minutes.

"I named this soup in honor of its open-a-can convenience. A quick sauté of onion and bell pepper provides a fresh base for the canned stuff that gets mixed in. Voila—it's done in minutes!"

French Onion Soup

4 servings

2   tablespoons butter

3   medium-sized sweet onions, thinly sliced

3   cups canned beef broth

1   tablespoon Worcestershire sauce

¼   teaspoon pepper

3   tablespoons dry sherry

4   (¾"-thick) slices French bread, toasted

½   cup (2 ounces) shredded Gruyère or Swiss cheese

1 Melt butter in a Dutch oven over medium-high heat. Add onions; sauté 5 minutes or just until tender. Add broth, Worcestershire, and pepper. Bring to a boil; cover, reduce heat, and simmer 20 minutes. Stir in sherry.

2 Preheat the oven to 300°. Ladle soup into individual 2-cup ovenproof bowls; place bowls on a baking sheet. Top each serving with a slice of bread. Sprinkle cheese evenly over bread. Bake at 300° for 10 minutes or until cheese melts. Use oven mitts to serve the hot bowls of soup.

❝ Sweet onions make the sweetest French onion soup. But some recipes sauté the sweet onions a little too long, which can make 'em gummy. My recipe gives 'em a quick sauté—just long enough to release their flavor—and then simmers 'em in the soup. How sweet it is!❞

Kielbasa and Black Bean Soup

4 cups

½   pound kielbasa, sliced
1   green, red, or yellow bell pepper,
      diced

1   (14-ounce) can chicken broth
1   (15-ounce) can black beans, rinsed
      and drained
¼   cup picante sauce or salsa
Chopped cilantro (optional)

1 Sauté kielbasa in a medium saucepan over medium-high heat until sausage begins to brown. Add bell pepper; sauté 1 minute.

2 Add broth; bring to a boil. Reduce heat to low; add beans and picante sauce, and simmer, covered, 5 minutes. Top each serving with cilantro, if desired.

> 66 *Kielbasa is just another name for Polish sausage. You'll love the way this smoked pork sausage adds robust flavor to this soup. If you're worried about fat and calories, try using turkey kielbasa instead of the traditional version.* 99

Spicy Vegetable Soup

12 cups

1   pound ground beef
1   medium onion, chopped
2   cloves garlic, pressed

1   (30-ounce) jar chunky spaghetti
       sauce with mushrooms and
       peppers
1   (10½-ounce) can beef broth,
       undiluted
2   cups water
1   teaspoon salt
½   teaspoon freshly ground black
       pepper
1   (10-ounce) can diced tomatoes
       and green chilies, undrained
1   (16-ounce) package frozen mixed
       vegetables

1 Cook first 3 ingredients in a large Dutch oven over medium heat, stirring until meat crumbles and is no longer pink. Drain and return to Dutch oven.

2 Add spaghetti sauce and remaining ingredients. Bring to a boil; cover, reduce heat, and simmer 10 minutes or until vegetables are tender, stirring often.

"I love to spice things up a bit with a can of diced tomatoes and green chilies. The chilies add a kick to this hearty soup that's chock-full of meat and veggies . . . and hearty enough as a meal all by itself!"

Italian Tomato-Corn Soup

(pictured on page 106)

4 cups

1   (10-ounce) package frozen
      whole kernel corn, thawed
2   teaspoons dried Italian seasoning
1   tablespoon roasted garlic-flavored
      vegetable oil (see tip below)

1   (14-ounce) can chicken broth
1   (10¾-ounce) can tomato soup,
      undiluted
½   teaspoon pepper

1 Sauté corn and Italian seasoning in hot oil in a large saucepan over medium-high heat 2 minutes.

2 Add broth and remaining ingredients. Bring to a boil; cover, reduce heat, and simmer 15 minutes.

Choices, Choices

The roasted garlic-flavored oil adds a robust flavor to the soup, but you can use a tablespoon of regular vegetable oil instead, along with a dash of garlic powder. Serve the soup with a grilled cheese sandwich, and you've got dinner!

Southwestern Chili

11 cups

1	pound ground chuck
1	large onion, chopped

3	cups water
2	(14½-ounce) cans diced chili-style tomatoes, undrained
2	(15-ounce) cans black beans, rinsed and drained
1	(16-ounce) jar picante sauce
½	teaspoon ground cumin

Shredded Cheddar cheese

1 Cook beef and onion in a Dutch oven, stirring until beef crumbles and is no longer pink; drain.

2 Stir in water and next 4 ingredients. Bring to a boil; reduce heat, and simmer, uncovered, 10 minutes, stirring occasionally. Sprinkle each serving with cheese.

"I've added black beans and picante sauce to this crowd-pleaser for south-of-the-border appeal. You can adjust the heat of the chili by using a hot, medium, or mild picante sauce. One bite of this chili and you'll shout 'Olé'!"

Crunchy Chicken Salad

4 servings

1	(3-ounce) package Oriental-flavored ramen noodles
½	cup slivered almonds
½	cup sunflower seeds
½	cup canola or vegetable oil
2	tablespoons sugar
2	tablespoons cider vinegar
2	roasted chicken breast halves, chopped (about 2⅓ cups)
1	(16-ounce) package coleslaw mix

1 Preheat the oven to 350°. Crumble uncooked noodles onto a baking sheet; set seasoning packet aside. Combine crumbled noodles with almonds and sunflower seeds on baking sheet. Bake at 350° for 7 to 8 minutes or until golden, stirring occasionally.

2 Combine seasoning packet, the oil, sugar, and vinegar in a jar. Cover tightly, and shake vigorously. Combine chicken, coleslaw mix, toasted noodle mixture, and dressing; toss well. Serve immediately.

A Meal-in-One Dish!
This easy one-dish meal makes good use of leftover chicken. If you prefer a meatless entrée, just omit the chicken—either way, you'll enjoy your crunchy creation.

Black-and-Blue Salad

(pictured on page 3)

6 servings

4   skinned and boned chicken breast
     halves
¼   cup Cajun seasoning

2   (6-ounce) packages mixed salad
     greens
2   slices red onion, chopped
2   large tomatoes, cut into wedges
16   peperoncini peppers
Bottled blue cheese dressing (see note
     below)

1 Spray both sides of chicken with
nonstick cooking spray for 5 seconds.
Coat chicken with Cajun seasoning.

2 Spray a large skillet with cooking
spray for 2 seconds, and heat skillet
over medium-high heat. Add seasoned
chicken, and cook 4 minutes on each
side. Remove chicken from skillet, and
cut into thin strips.

3 Toss together salad greens and next
3 ingredients in a large bowl; top
with chicken strips, and drizzle with blue
cheese dressing.

*My quick blackened chicken tossed into a green salad
and crowned with a 'bottled blue' makes a super salad supper.
It's even better with my homemade Roquefort Dressing on page 131,
but either way your gang's gonna love it! Serve it up with pita chips,
breadsticks, or focaccia wedges.*

Broccoli and Orange Salad

8 servings

¾ cup mayonnaise

¼ cup sugar

2 tablespoons white vinegar

1 (16-ounce) package broccoli florets

½ cup golden raisins

½ small red onion, thinly sliced and separated into rings

6 bacon slices, cooked and crumbled

1 (11-ounce) can mandarin oranges, drained

1 Stir together mayonnaise, sugar, and vinegar in a large bowl. Add broccoli and raisins; toss well. Cover and chill thoroughly.

2 Top with onion, crumbled bacon, and mandarin oranges.

Broccoli, red onion, bacon, raisins, and sweet mandarin oranges combine for a nice break from boring salad. This colorful salad works for potlucks and celebrations any time of year.

Raspberry-Spinach Salad

6 servings

2   tablespoons raspberry vinegar
2   tablespoons seedless raspberry jam
⅓   cup corn oil

4   cups torn fresh spinach, tightly
      packed (about 5 ounces)
1   (3.5-ounce) jar lightly salted
      macadamia nuts, chopped (about
      ½ cup)
1   cup fresh raspberries
3   kiwifruit, peeled and sliced

1 Process vinegar and jam in a blender until smooth, stopping to scrape down sides. With blender on high, gradually add oil in a slow, steady stream; blend until thickened.

2 Combine spinach and remaining 3 ingredients in a large bowl. Drizzle with dressing, and toss gently.

Get Dressed Quick!

The salad, that is! Keep close tabs on this quick little 3-ingredient dressing. You can vary the flavor simply by using different vinegars and jams to make a myriad of sweet-sour dressings at the punch of your blender's button!

Carrot "Waldorf" Salad

4 to 6 servings

5 carrots, peeled and grated
1 (8-ounce) can pineapple tidbits in
   heavy syrup, undrained
½ cup raisins
½ cup sliced celery
½ cup chopped walnuts
¼ cup mayonnaise
1 tablespoon lemon juice

1 Toss together all ingredients in a medium bowl. Cover and chill at least 1 hour before serving.

"Celery and walnuts add crunch, while raisins and pineapple sweeten this vitamin-packed salad. It's a play on the famous Waldorf salad, replacing the usual apple with colorful carrots."

Dilly-of-a-Pea Salad

6 servings

2   (10-ounce) packages frozen tiny
     green peas, thawed and drained
     (see note below)
1   (8-ounce) container sour cream
4   teaspoons lemon juice
1   green onion, sliced
2   teaspoons sugar
1   teaspoon chopped fresh dill
½   teaspoon salt
½   teaspoon curry powder
¼   teaspoon pepper

1 Combine all ingredients in a large bowl; toss gently. Cover and chill at least 1 hour before serving.

" I like to use those tiny, beautiful, bright green peas in this recipe. You can find 'em in the freezer section of your supermarket— but regular green peas work, too. "

Italian Tomato Salad

8 servings

4   large tomatoes, cut into ¼"-thick
       slices

4   to 5 cloves garlic, minced
½   cup chopped fresh parsley
¼   cup shredded fresh basil (see tip
       below)
½   cup olive oil
¼   cup water
½   teaspoon salt
1   teaspoon minced fresh oregano or
       ¼ teaspoon dried oregano
¼   teaspoon pepper

1 Arrange tomatoes in a 9" x 13" dish.

2 Stir together garlic and remaining 7 ingredients. Pour over tomato slices. Serve with slices of crusty Italian bread, if desired.

"Shear" Magic!
Try this easy way to shred fresh basil: Roll the leaves up together in a bundle and snip 'em with kitchen shears. Kitchen shears are the perfect tool for snipping all sorts of herbs, chopping canned tomatoes right in the can, or trimming the skin and fat from chicken and meat.

Freezer Slaw

6 to 8 servings

1½ cups sugar
1   cup cider vinegar

3   (10-ounce) packages shredded
       angel hair cabbage slaw
1   large carrot, peeled and shredded
1   small green bell pepper, diced
1   teaspoon celery salt
1   teaspoon mustard seeds (optional)

1 Bring sugar and vinegar to a boil in a small saucepan, stirring until sugar dissolves; cool.

2 Combine cabbage slaw and remaining 4 ingredients. Pour vinegar mixture over cabbage mixture, tossing to coat. Place in a large heavy-duty zip-top plastic bag or an airtight container, and freeze for up to 3 months. Thaw in refrigerator before serving.

Get a jump start on a holiday gathering with this make-ahead delight. Just toss the fixin's together and freeze! If you don't need to make it in advance, you can just cover and chill the slaw for at least 2 hours before serving.

Roquefort Dressing

(pictured on page 3)

2 cups

1 cup mayonnaise
4 ounces Roquefort cheese, crumbled (see note below)
½ cup buttermilk
1 tablespoon freshly ground pepper
1 tablespoon minced onion
2 tablespoons dry white wine
1 teaspoon minced garlic
1 teaspoon lemon juice

1 Combine all ingredients in a small bowl, stirring with a wire whisk until blended. Cover and chill. Serve over salad greens.

66 Don't be alarmed, my friends, about the generous amount of pepper in this recipe; it stands up nicely to the tangy Roquefort cheese. Oh—you can use blue cheese instead of Roquefort, if you'd like. 99

Poppy Seed Vinaigrette

¾ cup

½ cup vegetable oil
¼ cup sugar
¼ cup raspberry or red wine vinegar
   (see note below)
1 tablespoon poppy seeds
1 tablespoon minced onion
1 teaspoon dry mustard
½ teaspoon salt

1 Whisk together all ingredients in a bowl. Cover and chill. Whisk again just before serving over salad greens, grapefruit sections, or melon balls.

More and more flavors of vinegars keep popping up at the supermarket. You can use red wine, raspberry, or other fruit varieties in this family favorite. Splash a little on greens or fruit, and you've got a winner!

Breadshoppe Bounty

❝From breakfast pastries to dinner rolls, you can have homemade bread any day of the week with my no-fuss, 'I-can-do-it' recipes!❞

Easy Cheddar Biscuits

about 1 ½ dozen

1 ½ cups self-rising flour
1 tablespoon sugar
⅓ cup butter
½ cup milk
1 cup (4 ounces) shredded sharp
   Cheddar cheese

1 Preheat the oven to 425°. Combine flour and sugar in a large bowl. Cut in butter with a pastry blender or 2 knives until mixture is crumbly. Add milk, stirring just until moist. Stir in cheese.

2 Turn dough out onto a lightly floured surface. Knead with floured hands 3 or 4 times. Pat or roll dough to ½" thickness; cut with a 2" biscuit cutter. Place on a lightly greased baking sheet. Bake at 425° for 10 minutes or until golden.

❝ I've made these cheesy biscuits with both butter and butter-flavored shortening and loved 'em both. Use whatever's on hand!❞

Bacon Biscuit Cups

10 servings

2   (3-ounce) packages cream cheese, softened
2   tablespoons milk
1   large egg
½   cup (2 ounces) shredded Swiss cheese
1   green onion, chopped

1   (12-ounce) can refrigerated flaky biscuits
5   bacon slices, cooked and crumbled

1 Preheat the oven to 375°. Beat first 3 ingredients at medium speed of an electric beater until blended. Stir in cheese and green onion. Set aside.

2 Separate biscuits into 10 portions. Pat each portion into a 5" circle, and press on bottom and up sides of greased muffin cups, forming a ¼" crust edge. Sprinkle with half of bacon, and spoon cream cheese mixture on top.

3 Bake at 375° for 22 minutes or until set. Sprinkle with remaining bacon, lightly pressing into filling. Remove immediately from pan, and serve warm.

" To reheat any leftovers, wrap biscuit cups in foil, and bake 'em at 350° for 10 minutes or until warm. But I bet you won't have any extras! "

Ginger Scones

8 scones

2¾ cups all-purpose flour
2 teaspoons baking powder
½ teaspoon salt
½ cup sugar
¾ cup butter
⅓ cup chopped crystallized ginger
 (see note below)
1 cup milk

1 Preheat the oven to 400°. Combine first 4 ingredients in a large bowl; cut butter into flour mixture with a pastry blender until crumbly. Stir in ginger. Add milk, stirring just until dry ingredients are moistened.

2 Turn dough out onto a lightly floured surface, and knead with floured hands 10 to 15 times. Pat or roll dough to ¾" thickness on a lightly greased baking sheet; shape into a round, and cut dough into 8 wedges with a lightly floured knife, cutting into, but not through, dough.

3 Bake at 400° for 18 to 22 minutes or until just golden. Cool slightly on a wire rack. Serve warm.

"You may think these scones are fancy schmancy, but they're so-o-o easy! Here's a tip: Use cold butter to get a flaky result every time. Find crystallized ginger in the spice section of the supermarket. It adds texture and flavor to these scones that come out of the oven just beggin' to be savored with a cup of hot tea or coffee."

Out-of-This-World Waffles

22 (4") waffles

2½ cups all-purpose flour
1 tablespoon plus 1 teaspoon baking
  powder
¾ teaspoon salt
1½ tablespoons sugar

2 large eggs, beaten
2½ cups milk
¾ cup vegetable oil

1 Preheat the waffle iron. Combine first 4 ingredients in a large bowl.

2 Combine eggs, milk, and oil; add to flour mixture, stirring with a wire whisk just until dry ingredients are moistened.

3 Cook in oiled waffle iron until golden.

" These waffles are so crispy and light! If the recipe makes more waffles than you need, you can freeze and reheat 'em as needed in the toaster. And for more advice in a nutshell . . . you can add ½ cup of finely chopped pecans to the batter just before baking. "

Banana Pancakes with Peanut Butter and Jelly Syrups

12 (4") pancakes

2	cups biscuit mix
1	cup buttermilk
1	cup mashed banana
2	large eggs
½	teaspoon ground cinnamon
3	tablespoons butter
¾	cup maple syrup
¼	cup regular or reduced-fat peanut butter spread
Strawberry syrup	

1 Whisk together first 5 ingredients in a large bowl just until dry ingredients are moistened.

2 Melt 1 tablespoon butter on a hot griddle; pour about ¼ cup batter for each pancake onto griddle. Cook pancakes until tops are covered with bubbles; turn and cook other side of pancakes. Repeat procedure with remaining butter and pancake batter.

3 Whisk together maple syrup and peanut butter until smooth. Serve pancakes with peanut butter mixture and strawberry syrup.

" Watch out! Kids of all ages will love these pancakes with that classic flavor combo of PB & J. I like to serve 'em on the weekend for breakfast or even as a fast weeknight dinner. For fun pint-sized servings, try pouring 1 tablespoon of the batter per pancake on the hot griddle to make mini pancakes."

Painted French Toast

4 servings

6 large eggs
1 cup milk
Assorted liquid food colors

4 new small nontoxic paintbrushes
8 white bread slices

¼ cup butter

1 Whisk together eggs and milk. Pour ¼ cup egg mixture into each of 4 small bowls, reserving remaining mixture in a shallow dish. Add desired amount of a different food color to each bowl.

2 Paint each bread slice with desired colored egg mixture. Dip painted bread into reserved egg mixture.

3 Melt 2 tablespoons butter in a large skillet over medium-high heat; cook bread, in batches, 1½ minutes on each side or until browned. Repeat procedure with remaining butter and bread slices.

"My grandkids can't get enough of this one! We love to 'play with our food' and paint our way to breakfast. Let the kids choose their favorite colors to create their own French Toast masterpieces."

Cheddar Muffins

9 muffins

2	tablespoons butter, divided
½	cup chopped onion
1 ½	cups biscuit mix
1	cup (4 ounces) shredded sharp Cheddar cheese, divided
½	cup milk
1	large egg, beaten
1	tablespoon sesame seeds, toasted

1 Preheat the oven to 400°. Melt 1 tablespoon butter in a small skillet over medium-high heat. Add onion; sauté 3 minutes or until tender. Combine onion mixture, biscuit mix, and ½ cup cheese in a medium bowl; make a well in center of mixture. Combine milk and egg; pour into well, stirring just until moistened.

2 Spoon batter into greased muffin pans, filling half full. Sprinkle with remaining ½ cup cheese and the sesame seeds. Dot with remaining 1 tablespoon butter. Bake at 400° for 13 minutes or until muffins are golden. Remove from pans immediately.

" These cheesy muffins topped with golden sesame seeds will bring the bread basket center stage. Serve 'em warm straight from the oven and watch 'em disappear! "

Orange-Pecan Muffins

20 muffins

1	(3-ounce) package cream cheese, softened
¾	cup sugar
1	large egg

3	cups biscuit mix
1¼	cups orange juice
½	cup chopped pecans, toasted
1	teaspoon grated orange rind

1 Preheat the oven to 375°. Beat cream cheese at medium speed of an electric beater until fluffy, and gradually add sugar, beating well. Add egg, beating until blended.

2 Add biscuit mix to cream cheese mixture alternately with orange juice, beginning and ending with biscuit mix and beating after each addition. Stir in pecans and orange rind. Spoon batter into greased muffin pans, filling two-thirds full.

3 Bake at 375° for 22 minutes or until golden. Remove from pans immediately, and cool on wire racks.

" These easy muffins pair well with menus all year long. I love 'em for a brunch or in the springtime alongside vine-ripened tomatoes and chicken salad. No matter when you serve 'em, nobody will ever guess you used biscuit mix. Shhh ... it'll be our secret! "

Loaded Cornbread

9 servings

1 (12-ounce) package frozen corn soufflé, thawed
1 (8½-ounce) package Mexican cornbread mix
1 cup (4 ounces) shredded Cheddar cheese
8 bacon slices, cooked and crumbled
2 green onions, minced
¼ teaspoon ground red pepper

1 Preheat the oven to 400°. Stir together all ingredients until blended. Pour into a greased 8" square pan.

2 Bake at 400° for 28 minutes or until bread is lightly browned and a wooden toothpick inserted in center comes out clean. Cut into squares to serve.

Fry It Up!

Frying up crispy bacon shouldn't be a chore. To help separate the slices, remove the bacon from the fridge 30 minutes before cooking, or you can microwave it at HIGH 30 seconds. Start cooking bacon in a cold skillet, and cook over medium heat to minimize shrinkage. Also remember that the thinner the bacon, the crispier it becomes after frying.

Crispy Ranch Breadsticks

4 dozen

1   (11-ounce) can refrigerated
      breadsticks
Butter-flavored nonstick cooking spray
1   tablespoon dry Ranch dressing mix

1 Preheat the oven to 375°. Unroll breadsticks. Cut each breadstick in half crosswise, forming 3½" pieces; cut each portion in half lengthwise, forming ½" strips. Place on lightly greased baking sheets. Coat strips with nonstick cooking spray, and sprinkle with dressing mix.

2 Bake at 375° for 10 to 12 minutes or until lightly browned. Serve with spaghetti sauce.

" I like to serve these crispy breadsticks with warm spaghetti sauce, but they'd be great with a salad or your favorite dip. "

Italian "Parker House" Rolls

10 rolls

¾ cup Italian salad dressing (see tip below)

2 (12-ounce) cans refrigerated buttermilk biscuits

3 tablespoons grated Parmesan cheese

1 teaspoon poppy seeds

1 Preheat the oven to 400°. Pour dressing in a small bowl. Separate biscuits, and coat each with dressing. Fold biscuits in half. Place 2 biscuits, seam side down, into each of 10 lightly greased muffin pans.

2 Combine Parmesan cheese and poppy seeds, and sprinkle mixture evenly on biscuits.

3 Bake at 400° for 10 to 12 minutes or until golden.

Easy Way Out

This recipe simulates those tender, flaky 4-layer rolls by folding and pairing refrigerator biscuit dough in muffin pans. Be sure to use "real" Italian salad dressing rather than the diet kind because the latter may make the rolls soggy.

Onion-Bacon Rolls

2 dozen

8	bacon slices
1	small onion, diced
1	small green bell pepper, diced
½	teaspoon dried dillweed
½	teaspoon black pepper
1	(16-ounce) package frozen roll dough, thawed
¼	cup milk
2	teaspoons sesame seeds

1 Cook bacon in a large skillet until crisp; remove bacon, reserving 1 tablespoon drippings in skillet. Crumble bacon.

2 Sauté diced onion and bell pepper in drippings until tender; remove with a slotted spoon, and drain on paper towels. Place mixture in a small bowl; stir in bacon, dillweed, and black pepper.

3 Pat each roll into a 3" circle; spoon 1 tablespoon bacon mixture in center. Bring up edges, pinching to seal; place seam side down into lightly greased muffin pans.

4 Brush rolls with milk; sprinkle with sesame seeds. Cover and let rise in a warm place (85°), free from drafts, 30 minutes or until doubled in bulk.

5 Preheat the oven to 375°. Bake at 375° for 15 minutes or until golden.

“ Nothing calls the family to dinner quicker than the aroma of fresh baked bread. Prepare the rest of the meal and set the table while the rolls rise for 30 minutes. Once they've risen, you'll have mouthwatering homemade-tasting rolls after just 15 minutes in the oven. ”

Grilled Bread

6 servings

1 (18.5-ounce) package hoagie rolls, split
3 tablespoons olive oil
1 (4½-ounce) can chopped ripe olives, drained
6 plum tomatoes, thinly sliced
6 ounces Gruyère or Swiss cheese, shredded or sliced
⅓ cup coarsely chopped fresh basil

1 Preheat the grill. Brush cut sides of rolls with olive oil; sprinkle with olives. Top with tomato slices, cheese, and basil.

2 Coat cold grill rack with nonstick cooking spray; place rack on grill. Place rolls on rack, cut side up, and grill, covered, over medium heat (300° to 350°) 5 to 7 minutes or until cheese melts.

Grill the Whole Meal

Here's a great bread recipe to throw on the grill alongside any meat or poultry. Add the bread 5 minutes before everything else is done, and grill it just until the cheese melts.

Parmesan Cheese Bread

8 servings

1	(16-ounce) loaf French bread
2	cloves garlic, halved (see tip below)
6	tablespoons butter, softened
½	cup grated Parmesan cheese

1 Preheat the oven to 350°. Split bread loaf horizontally. Rub cut sides of loaf with garlic, and place bread on a baking sheet. Spread evenly with butter, and sprinkle with cheese.

2 Bake at 350° for 10 minutes or until toasted; cut into 2" slices.

Garlic Rub

Simply rubbing French bread with cut garlic imparts robust flavor without leaving chunks of garlic to bite into. Try this method with any kind of bread. The oil from the garlic transforms everyday bread into first-class fare!

Oat-Walnut Bread

1 loaf

1¼ cups very warm water
      (120° to 130°)
3 cups bread flour
1½ teaspoons salt
¼ cup packed brown sugar
½ cup quick-cooking oats
1 tablespoon butter
1½ teaspoons bread-machine yeast or
      rapid-rise yeast
¾ cup chopped walnuts (see note
      below)

1 Combine all ingredients in a bread machine according to manufacturer's instructions. Select bake cycle; start machine.

2 When baking is done, remove bread from pan; cool on a wire rack.

"This hearty bread is my favorite for the bread machine. Just set the dials and go have fun with the kids or grandkids. Be sure to check the instructions for your bread machine before adding the walnuts. Some machines require adding them at mid-cycle."

Basil Pesto Focaccia

(pictured on page 107)

6 to 8 servings

2 tablespoons cornmeal
1 (10-ounce) can refrigerated pizza
    crust

1 cup fresh basil (see tip below)
½ cup walnuts or pine nuts
1 tablespoon olive oil
1 clove garlic
¼ teaspoon salt
¼ teaspoon pepper

3 plum tomatoes, thinly sliced
½ cup (2 ounces) shredded provolone
    or Italian-blend cheeses

1 Preheat the oven to 450°. Sprinkle cornmeal onto a lightly greased baking sheet. Unroll pizza crust over cornmeal. Bake at 450° for 5 minutes or until golden brown.

2 Make pesto by processing basil and next 5 ingredients in a blender or food processor until blended, stopping to scrape down sides. Spread pesto evenly over crust.

3 Arrange tomato slices over pesto. Sprinkle with cheese.

4 Bake at 450° for 5 minutes or until cheese is melted. Cut into squares, and serve immediately.

No Time to Make Pesto?
No problem. Skip those ingredients, and use ⅓ cup prepared pesto instead. You'll find it with canned tomato products or pasta sauces in the supermarket.

Pecan Crescent Twists

8 servings

2   (8-ounce) cans refrigerated crescent
    rolls
6   tablespoons butter, melted and
    divided

½   cup chopped pecans
¼   cup sugar
1   teaspoon ground cinnamon

½   cup powdered sugar
2   tablespoons milk

1 Preheat the oven to 375°. Unroll crescent rolls, and separate each can into 4 rectangles, pressing perforations to seal. Brush with 4 tablespoons butter.

2 Stir together pecans, sugar, and cinnamon; sprinkle 1 tablespoon mixture on each rectangle, pressing in gently.

3 Roll up, starting at a long side, and twist. Cut 6 shallow (½"-long) diagonal slits in each roll; place on a lightly greased baking sheet. Brush twists with remaining 2 tablespoons butter. Bake at 375° for 12 minutes or until golden.

4 Stir together powdered sugar and milk until glaze is smooth; drizzle over warm twists.

“ I love to turn convenience products into culinary delights. Here I've taken canned crescent rolls, added some pecans, sugar, and cinnamon, and ended up with sweet breakfast pastries. A powdered sugar glaze tops the pastries for a final touch of sweetness. ”

Orange Breakfast Rolls

10 rolls

½ cup sugar
1 ½ teaspoons grated orange rind
½ teaspoon ground cinnamon

1 (12-ounce) can refrigerated
buttermilk biscuits
3 tablespoons fresh orange juice

1 Preheat the oven to 350°. Combine first 3 ingredients.

2 Dip each biscuit in orange juice, and dredge in sugar mixture.

3 Arrange biscuits in a lightly greased 9" round baking dish or cakepan. Sprinkle with remaining sugar mixture, and drizzle with remaining orange juice.

4 Bake at 350° for 25 minutes or until golden. Serve warm.

" For breakfast or an afternoon snack, you'll love to hear the gang beggin' for more of these oh-so-easy sweet rolls. "

Lazy Maple Sticky Buns

1 dozen

¼ cup packed brown sugar
¼ cup butter
2 tablespoons pure maple syrup
¼ cup chopped pecans

1 (8-ounce) can refrigerated crescent rolls
1 tablespoon granulated sugar
½ teaspoon ground cinnamon

1 Preheat oven to 375°. Combine brown sugar, butter, and syrup in an 8" round cakepan. Bake at 375° for 5 minutes or until butter melts; stir gently to blend ingredients. Sprinkle pecans over butter mixture.

2 Remove dough from package (do not unroll dough). Cut roll into 12 slices. Combine granulated sugar and cinnamon. Dip both sides of each slice of dough into sugar mixture. Arrange slices in prepared pan, cut side down. Sprinkle with remaining sugar mixture. Bake at 375° for 18 minutes or until golden. Invert pan immediately onto a serving platter. Serve immediately.

"These yummies get high marks for tastiness and innovative use of refrigerated rolls. And when they're inverted onto a serving plate, and that maple nut topping drenches the sweet rolls . . . watch out! They'll get grabbed up fast!"

Sweet Inspiration

"You'll keep everyone comin' back for more of these sweet treats that are a breeze to make.**"**

Apple Burritos

8 servings

1	(21-ounce) can apple pie filling
8	(6") flour tortillas

1½	cups apple cider
¾	cup sugar
¾	cup butter

1 Preheat the oven to 350°. Spoon about ⅓ cup pie filling onto each tortilla; roll up tortillas, and place seam side down in a lightly greased 7" x 11" baking dish.

2 Combine apple cider, sugar, and butter in a medium saucepan; bring to a boil. Reserve ½ cup sauce; pour remaining sauce over tortillas. Bake, covered, at 350° for 30 minutes. Uncover and bake 15 to 20 more minutes or until tortillas are lightly browned. Serve warm with reserved sauce.

" Juicy apple-filled tortilla wraps bake in a simple cider sauce. Top 'em off with a scoop of creamy vanilla ice cream or frozen yogurt for an over-the-top finale! "

Quick Doughnuts and Doughnut Holes

10 doughnuts and 10 doughnuts holes

1   (11-ounce) can refrigerated
      buttermilk biscuits

1   quart vegetable oil

1   cup sugar
1   tablespoon ground cinnamon
Chocolate Glaze (optional)

1 Separate biscuits, and place on a flat surface. Cut a hole from center of each biscuit with an apple corer, reserving dough balls.

2 Pour oil into a Dutch oven; heat to 350°. Fry doughnuts, in batches, 30 seconds on each side or until golden. Repeat procedure with dough balls. Remove with a slotted spoon, and drain on paper towels.

3 Combine sugar and cinnamon. Roll doughnuts and doughnut holes evenly in sugar mixture, or, if desired, dip in Chocolate Glaze.

Chocolate Glaze

¼   cup half-and-half
1   cup (6 ounces) semisweet chocolate
      chips
½   cup powdered sugar

1 Microwave half-and-half in a glass bowl at HIGH 1 minute or until hot. Add chocolate chips, stirring until smooth. Whisk in powdered sugar. Yield: ¾ cup.

" I really don't fry much anymore, but these bakery-style doughnuts are worth it! Your family will love you for 'em!"

Rocky Road Pizza Dessert

4 to 6 servings

1   (7") refrigerated pizza crust
¾   cup mini marshmallows
¾   cup candy-coated peanut butter
      pieces
¼   cup chopped pecans

1 Preheat the oven to 375°. Place crust on a baking sheet. Top evenly with marshmallows; sprinkle with candy pieces and pecans.

2 Bake at 375° for 10 to 15 minutes.

Pizza for dessert? You bet! Get the kids in on the action and let 'em make their own personalized creation. They can substitute their favorite candy as a topping, and they can even leave off the nuts, if they'd like. Chocolate or caramel sauce drizzled over the top is a crowd-pleaser every time. Anything will do!

Sweet Cherry Thing

15 servings

2½ cups crushed pecan shortbread
     cookies
½   cup butter

2   (21-ounce) cans cherry pie filling
1   teaspoon almond extract
1   teaspoon vanilla extract

1   (8-ounce) package cream cheese,
     softened
2   cups sifted powdered sugar
1   (12-ounce) container frozen
     whipped topping, thawed

1 Preheat the oven to 350°. Combine crushed cookies and butter with a pastry blender until mixture is crumbly. Press mixture into an ungreased 9" x 13" baking dish (see note below). Bake at 350° for 15 to 18 minutes or until lightly browned. Cool completely.

2 Meanwhile, stir together pie filling and almond and vanilla extracts in a large bowl; set aside.

3 Beat cream cheese and powdered sugar at medium speed of an electric beater until creamy; fold in whipped topping. Spoon into cooled crust. Top with pie filling mixture, spreading evenly. Cover and chill at least 8 hours. Cut into squares to serve.

> " *After pouring the crumb mixture into the baking dish, place a large piece of plastic wrap over it, and press the crumbs into the dish. Remove the plastic wrap and your crust is evenly packed—no messy hands!* "

Raspberry Cloud

6 servings

3   pints raspberries (see tip below)

½   cup heavy whipping cream
½   cup sour cream
2   tablespoons sugar
1   tablespoon lemon juice

1 Spoon raspberries evenly into 6 dessert glasses.

2 Combine whipping cream and remaining ingredients; stir well. Spoon cream mixture over berries, and serve immediately.

Berry, Berry Good

You can usually substitute berries in simple dessert recipes such as this one, so feel free to use what's in season. Sliced strawberries would be great here, or try any combination of blueberries, blackberries, and raspberries . . . the possibilities are endless!

No-Fuss Chocolate Mousse

5 servings

5   (1-ounce) semisweet chocolate
     squares, chopped
1 ¼ cups whipping cream

1 Combine chocolate and whipping cream in a heavy saucepan. Cook over medium-low heat, stirring constantly, until chocolate melts and mixture is smooth. Remove from heat, and cool completely. Transfer mixture to a mixing bowl; cover and chill at least 8 hours.

2 Just before serving, beat chocolate mixture at medium-high speed of an electric beater until mixture thickens to desired consistency. Spoon into individual dessert dishes.

For Adults Only

For an added flavor boost, stir 1 to 2 teaspoons coffee liqueur or orange liqueur into the melted chocolate mixture.

Strawberry Mousse

6 servings

1½ cups fresh strawberries (about 16 small)
1   (8-ounce) package cream cheese, cut into cubes and softened
½   cup sifted powdered sugar
½   (8-ounce) container frozen whipped topping, thawed (1¾ cups)

Toasted sliced natural almonds

1 Process first 3 ingredients in a food processor until smooth. Transfer mixture to a large bowl; fold in whipped topping.

2 Spoon berry mixture into 6 (6-ounce) dessert dishes. Cover and chill at least 3 hours or up to 8 hours. Sprinkle with almonds just before serving.

Ooh la la!
Add instant refinement to this smooth strawberry pleaser by serving it in your fanciest stemmed wine glasses.

Black-Bottom Ice Cream Shake

4 servings

¾   cup chocolate flavor syrup
1   quart vanilla ice cream, softened
1½   cups milk
1   tablespoon instant coffee granules

Shaved chocolate (optional)
      (see page 165 for how-to)

1 Spoon 3 tablespoons chocolate syrup into each of 4 tall glasses. Place ice cream in a large bowl. Stir ice cream to soften; quickly stir in milk and coffee.

2 Pour over chocolate syrup in glasses. Sprinkle with shaved chocolate, if desired.

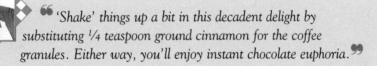

" 'Shake' things up a bit in this decadent delight by substituting ¼ teaspoon ground cinnamon for the coffee granules. Either way, you'll enjoy instant chocolate euphoria. "

Easy Pudding Shake

5 cups

3 cups milk
1½ cups chocolate ice cream, softened
1 (3.4-ounce) package chocolate
  instant pudding mix

1 Process all ingredients in a blender on low until smooth, stopping to scrape down sides. (Blender will be very full.)

2 Serve immediately, or cover and chill up to 8 hours. Stir well before serving.

" Kids will love this easy shake. For variety and excitement, use different flavors of pudding and ice cream each time you make it. "

1-2-3 Blackberry Sherbet

4 cups

4   cups fresh blackberries (see note
    below)

2   cups sugar

2   cups buttermilk

Blackberries and fresh mint (optional)

1 Stir together blackberries and sugar in a bowl; let stand 30 minutes.

2 Process blackberry mixture in a blender or food processor until smooth, stopping to scrape down sides. Pour through a fine wire-mesh strainer into a 9" square pan, discarding solids; stir in buttermilk. Cover and freeze 8 hours.

3 Break frozen mixture into chunks, and place in bowl; beat at medium speed of an electric beater until smooth. Return to pan; cover and freeze 3 hours or until firm. Garnish with extra blackberries and mint, if desired.

" You can substitute 2 (14-ounce) packages frozen blackberries, thawed, for the fresh, if you'd like. "

Chocolate Cookie Ice Cream

13 cups

1   (16-ounce) package cream-filled
     chocolate sandwich cookies,
     coarsely crumbled (42 cookies)
½   gallon vanilla ice cream, slightly
     softened
1   (8-ounce) container frozen whipped
     topping, thawed

1 Combine crumbled cookies and softened ice cream, stirring just until
blended. Fold in whipped topping.
Spoon mixture into a 9" x 13" pan or
other shallow container.

2 Cover and freeze until firm. Scoop
into serving bowls.

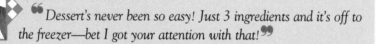

*" Dessert's never been so easy! Just 3 ingredients and it's off to
the freezer—bet I got your attention with that!"*

Mint-Chocolate Chip Ice-Cream Cupcakes

12 cupcakes

1   (19.8-ounce) package fudge
      brownie mix
½   cup water
½   cup vegetable oil
3   large eggs

½   gallon mint-chocolate chip ice
      cream, softened

1   (8-ounce) container frozen whipped
      topping, thawed

½   (4.67-ounce) package chocolate
      mints

1 Preheat the oven to 350°. Stir together first 4 ingredients until blended. Place 12 foil baking cups into muffin pans; spoon batter into cups.

2 Bake at 350° for 20 to 25 minutes. (A wooden toothpick inserted in center will not come out clean.) Cool in pans on wire racks 10 minutes; remove from pans, and cool completely on wire racks.

3 Return cupcakes to muffin pans, and spoon ice cream over each. Freeze 8 hours or until firm.

4 Dollop whipped topping over ice cream. Freeze until ready to serve.

5 Pull a vegetable peeler down sides of mints, making tiny curls; sprinkle curls over cupcakes just before serving.

66 Who says you can't have your cake and ice cream, too? Your kids will come runnin' for these minty cool treats. Make 'em ahead and store 'em in the freezer up to 2 weeks for spur-of-the-moment snack attacks! 99

Hot Fudge Sauce

3 cups

2   (14-ounce) cans sweetened
     condensed milk
1   cup (6 ounces) semisweet chocolate
     chips
Dash of salt
2   teaspoons vanilla extract

1 Combine first 3 ingredients in a heavy saucepan, and cook over medium-low heat 4 to 6 minutes or until smooth, stirring constantly. Remove from heat; stir in vanilla. Use immediately or store covered in refrigerator and reheat just before serving.

"Wanna leave a lasting impression? Then dress up store-bought cake, pie, or ice cream with this too-good-to-resist sauce. It's a chocolate dream!"

Extra-Easy Chocolate Pie

6 to 8 servings

1 (7-ounce) milk chocolate bar with almonds
2 tablespoons water
1 (8-ounce) container frozen whipped topping, thawed
1 (6-ounce) graham cracker pie crust

1 Combine chocolate and water in a microwave-safe bowl. Microwave at MEDIUM (50% power) 1½ to 2 minutes; stir until smooth. Fold in whipped topping; pour into crust.

2 Cover and chill at least 8 hours before serving.

This recipe gives new meaning to the phrase 'easy as pie'! Just zap 2 ingredients in the microwave, fold in whipped topping, pour filling into a graham cracker pie crust, and chill overnight. Voila!

Lemon Pie—Oh My!

6 to 8 servings

1   (14-ounce) can sweetened
       condensed milk

¼   cup fresh lemon juice (about 2
       lemons)

1   cup whipping cream, whipped

1   (6-ounce) graham cracker pie crust

1 Fold condensed milk and lemon juice into whipped cream; pour into crust.

2 Cover and chill 4 hours or until firm.

"No time to make dessert? There is with this creamy concoction bursting with lemony flavor. You're just 4 ingredients and 2 steps away from having 'em screamin' 'OOH IT'S SO GOOD!!'"

Espresso Ice Cream Pie

6 to 8 servings

½ cup chocolate-covered coffee beans, divided (see note below)
4 cups vanilla ice cream, softened
1 (6-ounce) chocolate crumb pie crust

Caramel sauce
Fresh raspberries (optional) (about 1 pint)

1 Process ¼ cup coffee beans in a blender until finely chopped. Add ice cream; process until smooth, stopping to scrape down sides. Spoon mixture into crust; cover and freeze at least 2 hours.

2 Drizzle with caramel sauce. Sprinkle with remaining coffee beans, and garnish with raspberries, if desired.

❝You can find chocolate-covered coffee beans at your favorite gourmet coffee shop. They add rich, robust flavor and crunch to this foolproof pie.❞

Gingersnap Streusel Pumpkin Pie

6 servings

1   (3-pound 1-ounce) package frozen
      pumpkin custard pie

10 gingersnaps, coarsely crushed
⅓   cup honey-roasted almonds,
      chopped
2   tablespoons all-purpose flour
2   tablespoons light brown sugar
2   tablespoons butter, softened
¼   teaspoon ground cinnamon

1 Preheat the oven to 400°. Remove and discard paper circle from pie. Place frozen pie on a heavy baking sheet. Bake at 400° for 30 minutes. Remove from oven.

2 Stir together crushed gingersnaps and remaining 5 ingredients until crumbly; sprinkle over pie.

3 Bake at 400° for 1 hour, shielding top of pie with aluminum foil after 30 minutes (see tip below).

Shield That Pie!

It's always best to shield your pie crust about halfway into its baking time. This will protect the crust edges from overbrowning. Cut out a square of aluminum foil large enough to cover the pie. Cut the center out of the square, and mold the foil ring around the edges of the pie. You'll have a golden crust every time.

Mocha Mud Pie

6 to 8 servings

1 cup hot fudge sauce, divided
1 (13¾-ounce) package macaroon
    cookies, crumbled
1 quart chocolate fudge ice cream,
    slightly softened

1 quart coffee ice cream, slightly
    softened
Crushed toffee candy bars (optional)

1 Microwave ½ cup fudge sauce in a glass bowl at HIGH 20 seconds. Press half of crumbled cookies in a greased 9" springform pan. Spread chocolate ice cream over cookie crumbs. Drizzle warm fudge sauce over ice cream. Sprinkle with remaining cookie crumbs. Cover and freeze at least 1 hour.

2 Microwave remaining ½ cup fudge sauce in glass bowl at HIGH 20 seconds. Spread coffee ice cream over cookie crumb layer. Drizzle with sauce. Sprinkle with crushed candy, if desired. Cover and freeze 4 hours or until firm. Remove sides from pan; transfer pie to a serving plate.

❝ The flavors of chocolate, toffee, macaroons, and coffee mingle in this showstopping finale. I guarantee they'll be comin' back for seconds!❞

Banana Cream-Crunch Pie

(pictured on facing page)

6 to 8 servings

1   (3.4-ounce) package banana cream-
     flavored instant pudding mix
1   cup milk
5   tablespoons coffee liqueur, divided
     (see note below)
1   (8-ounce) container frozen whipped
     topping, thawed and divided

2   bananas, sliced
1   (6-ounce) chocolate graham cracker
     pie crust
3   (1.4-ounce) toffee candy bars,
     chopped

1 Combine pudding mix, milk, and 4 tablespoons liqueur in a medium bowl, stirring with a wire whisk until smooth. Gently fold 1 cup whipped topping into pudding mixture.

2 Toss banana slices with remaining 1 tablespoon liqueur, and arrange over crust. Sprinkle with half of the chopped candy. Spoon pudding mixture over chopped candy. Cover and chill 1 ½ hours or until set. Spoon remaining whipped topping on top of pie just before serving. Sprinkle with remaining chopped candy.

Leave out the liqueur if you want a more kid-friendly dessert. Either way you slice it, you'll have a hit!

Double Chocolate Chewies,
page 185

Peanut Butter Swirl Bars,
page 194

Quick Italian Cream Cake

(pictured on facing page)

16 servings

1　(18.25-ounce) package white cake mix with pudding
3　large eggs
1 ¼　cups buttermilk
¼　cup vegetable oil
1　(3½-ounce) can flaked coconut
1 ⅔　cups chopped pecans, toasted and divided

3　tablespoons rum (optional)

2　(12-ounce) containers cream cheese frosting

1 Preheat the oven to 350°. Beat first 4 ingredients at medium speed of an electric beater 2 minutes. Stir in coconut and ⅔ cup pecans. Pour into 3 greased and floured 9" round cakepans.

2 Bake at 350° for 15 to 17 minutes or until a wooden toothpick inserted in center comes out clean. Cool in pans on wire racks 10 minutes. Remove from pans, and cool completely on wire racks.

3 Sprinkle each cake layer with rum, if desired; let stand 10 minutes.

4 Stir together frosting and remaining 1 cup toasted pecans. Spread frosting between layers and on top and sides of cake. Chill 2 hours before slicing.

Frosting Basics

Always cool the cake layers completely and brush away excess crumbs before frosting. Stack the first 2 layers on a serving plate, bottom side up; then place the top layer right side up. This will make a straight and tall cake. Spread a thin layer of frosting on the sides to set any crumbs, then spread frosting generously on the sides and tops. And there—you've got a perfect layer cake!

Chocolate-Raspberry Cake

(pictured on page 4)

12 servings

1   (18.25-ounce) package Swiss
    chocolate cake mix without
    pudding
3   large eggs
½   cup vegetable oil
1⅓ cups water

¼   cup seedless raspberry jam

½   cup whipping cream
1   cup (6 ounces) semisweet chocolate
    chips

1 Preheat the oven to 350°. Beat first 4 ingredients at medium speed of an electric beater 2 minutes. Pour batter into 3 greased and floured 8" round cakepans.

2 Bake at 350° for 15 to 20 minutes or until a wooden toothpick inserted in center comes out clean. Cool in pans on wire racks 10 minutes; remove from pans, and cool completely on wire racks.

3 Spread 2 tablespoons raspberry jam between the layers.

4 Place whipping cream in a microwave-safe bowl. Microwave at HIGH 1 minute; add chocolate chips, stirring until chips melt and the mixture is smooth. Let chocolate mixture stand 45 minutes or until spreading consistency. Spread chocolate mixture on top and sides of cake. Chill until ready to serve. Garnish with whipped cream, fresh mint sprigs, and raspberries, if desired.

"Who would ever guess a three-layer chocolate cake could be so easy! Shhh! My secret is a Swiss chocolate cake mix whipped up in a hurry. Raspberry jam moistens each cake layer, and a decadent chocolate frosting crowns the treat. It's love at first bite!"

Banana Pudding Cake

14 servings

1	(18.25-ounce) package yellow cake mix
1	(3.4-ounce) package vanilla instant pudding mix
4	large eggs
1	cup water
½	cup mashed ripe banana (about 1 medium)
¼	cup vegetable oil

1 Preheat the oven to 350°. Combine all ingredients in a large mixing bowl. Beat at medium speed of an electric beater until blended. Pour into a greased 10" tube pan.

2 Bake at 350° for 50 to 55 minutes or until a wooden toothpick inserted in center comes out clean. Cool in pan on a wire rack 15 minutes; remove from pan, and cool completely on wire rack.

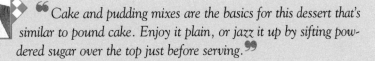

Cake and pudding mixes are the basics for this dessert that's similar to pound cake. Enjoy it plain, or jazz it up by sifting powdered sugar over the top just before serving.

Layered Strawberry Cake

12 servings

1   (18.25-ounce) package butter recipe
        golden cake mix
⅔   cup buttermilk
½   cup butter, softened
3   large eggs

½   cup strawberry preserves, divided

2   cups whipping cream
3   tablespoons powdered sugar

2   quarts fresh strawberries, sliced

1 Preheat the oven to 350°. Beat first 4 ingredients at low speed of an electric beater until cake mix is moistened. Beat at medium speed 4 minutes. Pour batter into 2 greased and floured 9" round cakepans.

2 Bake at 350° for 18 to 20 minutes or until a wooden toothpick inserted in center comes out clean. Cool on wire racks 10 minutes; remove from pans. Brush top of each layer with 2 tablespoons preserves. Cool completely on wire racks.

3 Beat remaining preserves with whipping cream and powdered sugar at high speed of an electric beater until stiff peaks form.

4 Place 1 cake layer on a serving plate. Arrange half of strawberries over layer; top with half of whipped cream mixture. Repeat procedure with remaining layer, strawberries, and whipped cream mixture. Garnish with extra strawberries, if desired.

❝Don't be intimidated by layer cakes. You'll have this showy strawberry cake whipped up in no time flat, and the result . . . it's oh-so out of this world!❞

Brown Sugar Snack Cake

15 servings

1½ cups biscuit mix
1   (16-ounce) package light brown
      sugar
4   large eggs, lightly beaten
1   teaspoon vanilla extract
1   cup flaked coconut
1   cup chopped pecans (optional)

1 Preheat the oven to 350°. Stir together biscuit mix and brown sugar. Add eggs, and beat with a spoon until blended. Stir in vanilla, coconut, and, if desired, pecans. Pour into a lightly greased 9" x 13" pan.

2 Bake at 350° for 30 minutes or until a wooden toothpick inserted in center comes out clean. Cool in pan on a wire rack. Cut into squares to serve.

"I love snack cakes because they're a snap to make and they're a hit every time with everybody. My secret with this cake is biscuit mix that gives it a texture similar to chewy brownies. Mmm!"

Frozen Peppermint Cheesecake

12 servings

1¼ cups chocolate wafer crumbs (about 25 wafers)

¼ cup sugar

¼ cup butter, melted

1 (8-ounce) package cream cheese, softened

1 (14-ounce) can sweetened condensed milk

1 cup crushed hard peppermint candy

2 cups whipping cream

1 Stir together first 3 ingredients; press mixture in bottom and 1" up sides of a 9" springform pan. Set aside.

2 Beat cream cheese at medium speed of an electric beater until creamy. Gradually add milk, beating until smooth. Stir in candy.

3 Beat whipping cream until soft peaks form; gently fold whipped cream into cream cheese mixture. Pour into prepared pan. Cover and freeze 6 hours or until firm. Remove sides of pan just before serving.

"Wake up your taste buds with this no-bake cheesecake that explodes with big peppermint flavor. For a classic pairing, serve slices in generous puddles of rich chocolate sauce, and sit back and enjoy the raves!"

Cookie Jar Jubilee

“Betcha no one will be able to resist these freshly baked cookies and ooh-so-sweet candies!”

Almond Lace Cookies

about 2½ dozen

¾   cup sugar
¼   cup all-purpose flour
2½ cups sliced almonds
1   egg white, lightly beaten
⅓   cup butter, melted
1   teaspoon vanilla extract

1 Preheat the oven to 350°. Stir together first 3 ingredients in a large bowl; stir in egg white, butter, and vanilla until blended. Drop dough by tablespoonfuls onto parchment paper-lined baking sheets (see tip below).

2 Bake at 350° for 10 to 12 minutes or until golden. Cool on baking sheets. Remove from paper, and store in an airtight container.

Lining Lesson

For most cookies, don't worry about lining the baking sheet with parchment paper, but in this case it will help in removing the delicate almond cookies from the pan after baking. You can usually find parchment paper near aluminum foil in the supermarket.

Double Chocolate Chewies

(pictured on page 174)

about 5½ dozen

¾ cup butter, softened
1½ cups sugar
2 large eggs
1 cup all-purpose flour
¾ cup cocoa
1 teaspoon baking powder
2 cups (12 ounces) semisweet
    chocolate chips
1 cup coarsely chopped pecans,
    toasted

1 Preheat the oven to 350°. Beat butter and sugar at medium speed of an electric beater until creamy. Add eggs and next 3 ingredients, beating until blended. Stir in chocolate chips and pecans. Drop mixture by heaping table-spoonfuls onto ungreased baking sheets.

2 Bake at 350° for 8 to 9 minutes. (Tops will be soft.) Cool cookies on baking sheets 1 minute; remove to wire racks to cool completely.

" These gooey chocolate treats are perfect with a tall glass of milk. Don't overbake 'em unless you prefer a crisp cookie."

Nutty Chocolate Chippers

about 4½ dozen

1   (18.25-ounce) package chocolate or
      yellow cake mix
½   cup vegetable oil
2   large eggs

1   cup (6 ounces) semisweet chocolate
      chips
½   cup chopped pecans

1 Preheat the oven to 350°. Beat first 3 ingredients at medium speed of an electric beater until smooth.

2 Stir in chocolate chips and pecans. Drop by heaping teaspoonfuls onto ungreased baking sheets.

3 Bake at 350° for 8 to 10 minutes or until lightly browned. Remove to wire racks to cool completely.

Drop-Dead Delicious Cookies!

When making drop cookies, use a teaspoon (not a measuring spoon) to pick up the dough and use another one to push the dough onto the baking sheet. Try to scoop equal amounts so the cookies will be the same size. Leave 1" to 2" between dough balls so they won't run together when they bake. You'll have delicious cookies in no time!

Chocolate Cappuccino Cookies

about 8 dozen

2 cups butter, softened
4 cups packed light brown sugar
4 large eggs

5½ cups all-purpose flour
1 cup cocoa
¼ cup instant coffee granules
1 teaspoon baking powder
1 teaspoon baking soda
1 teaspoon salt
1⅔ cups (10 ounces) cinnamon
     chocolate chips (see note below)

1 Preheat the oven to 350°. Beat butter at medium speed of an electric beater until creamy. Gradually add brown sugar, beating well. Add eggs, beating until blended.

2 Combine flour and next 5 ingredients. Gradually add to butter mixture, beating at low speed just until blended. Stir in cinnamon chips.

3 Drop dough by rounded tablespoonfuls 2" apart onto lightly greased baking sheets.

4 Bake at 350°, in batches, for 8 to 10 minutes per batch. Cool on baking sheets 5 minutes. Remove to wire racks to cool completely.

You can substitute 1⅔ cups chocolate chips tossed with 1 teaspoon of ground cinnamon for the cinnamon chips, if you'd like. I always like to use what's on hand in my pantry to make things oh-so-easy!

Chocolate Mint Surprise Cookies

about 4 dozen

1 cup butter, softened
1 cup sugar
½ cup packed brown sugar
2 large eggs
1 teaspoon vanilla extract

3 cups all-purpose flour
1 teaspoon baking soda
½ teaspoon salt

2 (4.67-ounce) packages chocolate mint wafer candies

1 Preheat the oven to 375°. Beat butter at medium speed of an electric beater until creamy; gradually add sugars, beating well. Add eggs, 1 at a time, beating until blended after each addition. Stir in the vanilla.

2 Combine flour, baking soda, and salt; add to butter mixture, beating well.

3 Drop dough by teaspoonfuls 2" apart onto ungreased baking sheets. Press 1 candy on top of each mound of dough; cover each with 1 teaspoonful of dough. Bake at 375° for 11 minutes or until golden. Remove immediately to wire racks to cool completely.

" Cool mint chocolate candies hide inside these cookies for an unexpected flavor bonus. It's no surprise that they'll be a hit with any crowd!"

Marvelous Macaroons

about 2 dozen

2⅔ cups shredded coconut
⅔ cup sugar
¼ cup all-purpose flour
¼ teaspoon salt
4 egg whites
1 teaspoon almond extract
1 cup slivered almonds

1 Preheat the oven to 325°. Combine first 4 ingredients in a medium bowl; stir well. Add egg whites and almond extract; stir well. Stir in almonds.

2 Drop dough by teaspoonfuls onto greased baking sheets. Bake at 325° for 22 minutes or until golden. Remove immediately to wire racks to cool completely.

" These quick confections are an old-fashioned favorite that never goes out of style. Mix 'em up in a bowl, drop 'em onto baking sheets, and just pop 'em in the oven. You can't get much easier than that! "

189

Lemon Whippers

about 5 dozen

1 (18.25-ounce) package lemon
   cake mix

2 cups frozen whipped topping,
   thawed

1 large egg, lightly beaten

Powdered sugar (about 1 cup)

1 Preheat the oven to 350°. Combine first 3 ingredients in a large bowl, stirring well.

2 Shape dough into balls, using 1 teaspoon of dough for each; roll in powdered sugar. Place on greased baking sheets.

3 Bake at 350° for 8 to 10 minutes or until edges are golden. Cool 1 minute on baking sheets; remove to wire racks to cool completely.

❝ This recipe makes plenty of sugar-coated balls, so you'll have enough for a cookie exchange or for gift giving. They'll win 'oohs' and 'aahs' every time! ❞

Chocolate Shortbreads

about 3½ dozen

2   cups all-purpose flour
1   cup sifted powdered sugar
½   cup unsweetened cocoa
¼   teaspoon salt
1   cup cold butter, diced
1   teaspoon vanilla extract

1 Preheat the oven to 300°. Process first 4 ingredients in a food processor until blended. Add butter and vanilla; process until mixture forms a ball, stopping to scrape down sides.

2 Roll dough to ¼" thickness on a lightly floured surface; cut into 1" x 3½" strips, using a fluted pastry cutter or sharp knife. Place 1" apart on ungreased baking sheets. Bake strips at 300° for 18 to 22 minutes. Cool 1 minute on baking sheets; remove to wire racks to cool completely.

On a Roll!
No fancy cookie cutters for these wavy, shapely shortbread cookies. Just roll out the dough and whip out a fluted pastry cutter to cut wavy-edged cookies in record time.

Mini Pecan Tassies

40 mini tassies

1	cup packed brown sugar
½	cup butter, melted
2	large eggs
1	teaspoon vanilla extract
1	cup chopped pecans
½	cup all-purpose flour

1 Preheat the oven to 375°. Combine first 4 ingredients in a bowl, beating with a wire whisk until smooth. Stir in pecans and flour. Spoon batter into miniature (1¾") muffin pans coated with nonstick cooking spray, filling to within ⅛" from top.

2 Bake at 375° for 12 minutes or until lightly browned. Cool in pans on wire racks 1 minute. Remove from pans; cool completely on wire racks.

" My mini tassies are easier to prepare than most because there's no separate crust. Betcha can't eat just one!"

Apple-Oat Snack Squares

about 16 squares

3	cups biscuit mix
2	cups uncooked quick-cooking oats
⅔	cup packed light brown sugar
1	teaspoon ground cinnamon
½	cup butter, cut into pieces
1	cup milk
1	(21-ounce) can apple pie filling
2	tablespoons light brown sugar

1 Preheat the oven to 350°. Stir together first 4 ingredients in a medium bowl; cut in butter with a pastry blender until crumbly. Stir in milk just until dry ingredients are moistened. Fold in pie filling, and spoon into a lightly greased 9" x 13" pan. Sprinkle with 2 tablespoons brown sugar.

2 Bake at 350° for 40 minutes or until golden. Cool on a wire rack, and cut into squares.

Break out these cakelike squares for the after-school gang. Serve 'em up with tall glasses of milk and watch 'em disappear.

Peanut Butter Swirl Bars

(pictured on page 175)

about 2 dozen

½ cup chunky peanut butter
⅓ cup butter, softened
¾ cup packed brown sugar
¾ cup granulated sugar
2   large eggs
2   teaspoons vanilla extract

1   cup self-rising flour
2   cups (12 ounces) semisweet
     chocolate chips

1 Preheat the oven to 350°. Beat first 4 ingredients at medium speed of an electric beater until creamy. Add eggs and vanilla; beat well.

2 Add flour to butter mixture, beating well. Spread batter in an ungreased 9" x 13" pan. Sprinkle with chocolate chips. Bake at 350° for 5 minutes. Remove from oven. Run a knife through batter to swirl chocolate. Return to oven; bake 30 more minutes. Cool completely in pan on a wire rack. Cut into bars.

These little bar cookies look so fancy, but they're a cinch to swirl—you'll see!

Toffee Cookie Bars

about 2 dozen

½ cup butter

1½ cups graham cracker crumbs (about 12 rectangle crackers)
1 (14-ounce) can sweetened condensed milk
1¼ cups almond toffee bits
1¼ cups English toffee bits or crushed English toffee candy bars
1 cup (6 ounces) semisweet chocolate chips
1½ cups chopped pecans

1 Preheat the oven to 325°. Place butter in a 9" x 13" baking dish; heat at 325° for 4 minutes or until butter melts.

2 Layer graham cracker crumbs and remaining 5 ingredients in baking dish with melted butter. Firmly press mixture in dish.

3 Bake at 325° for 25 minutes or until edges are lightly browned. Cool completely in dish on a wire rack. Cut into bars.

"Now here's what I call a real one-dish recipe! No mixing bowl to wash—just melt the butter right in the pan and layer on all the goods!"

Mint Julep Brownies

about 2 dozen

1	cup butter
4	(1-ounce) unsweetened chocolate squares
4	large eggs
2	cups sugar
1½	cups all-purpose flour
½	teaspoon salt
2	tablespoons bourbon (see note below)
1	teaspoon peppermint extract

1 Preheat the oven to 350°. Melt butter and chocolate in a heavy saucepan over low heat, stirring until smooth; cool slightly. Beat eggs at medium speed of an electric beater 2 minutes. Gradually add sugar, beating well. Add the chocolate mixture, flour, and remaining 3 ingredients; beat well. Pour batter into a greased and floured 9" x 13" pan.

2 Bake at 350° for 25 to 30 minutes. Cool completely in pan on a wire rack. Cut into bars.

For a truly sinful dessert experience, serve these bourbon-spiked brownies warm, topped with a dainty scoop or two of mint chocolate chip ice cream. Just remember—they're for adults only!

Chocolate Sandwich Cookie Truffles

about 3 dozen

1   (4-ounce) sweet chocolate bar
20 cream-filled chocolate sandwich
      cookies, crushed (about 2 cups
      crumbs)
1   cup toasted almonds, ground
3   tablespoons whipping cream
3   tablespoons orange juice
1   tablespoon finely chopped orange
      rind

Toppings: powdered sugar, ground
      toasted almonds, unsweetened
      cocoa

1 Melt chocolate in a heavy saucepan over low heat, stirring until smooth. Remove from heat; stir in cookie crumbs and next 4 ingredients. Shape mixture into 1" balls, washing hands as necessary. Cover and chill 20 minutes.

2 Roll 1 dozen balls in powdered sugar, 1 dozen in ground almonds, and 1 dozen in cocoa. Store in an airtight container in refrigerator.

❝ Your favorite cream-filled chocolate sandwich cookies get all dressed up and transformed into decadent truffles. Roll 'em in a variety of toppings for an oh-so-lovely presentation. Invite your friends over for coffee, and enjoy! ❞

Robin's Nests

about 20 cookies

1   (7-ounce) bag sweetened flaked coconut

3   tablespoons sugar

⅔   cup (4 ounces) semisweet chocolate chips

2   egg whites

1   teaspoon vanilla extract

⅛   teaspoon salt

60   pastel jelly beans

1 Stir together coconut and sugar in a large bowl. Set aside. Microwave chocolate chips in a microwave-safe 1-quart bowl at HIGH 1½ minutes, stirring twice. Let stand on counter to cool slightly.

2 Preheat the oven to 350°. Whisk together egg whites, vanilla, and salt. Stir in melted chocolate. Pour into coconut mixture, stirring well.

3 Line baking sheets with lightly greased parchment paper. Drop coconut mixture by heaping tablespoonfuls 2" apart onto prepared baking sheets. Make an indentation in the middle of each mound with thumb to form a nest.

4 Bake at 350° for 14 minutes or until bottoms are crisp. (Centers will be soft.) Remove from oven; press 3 jelly beans into center of each nest. Cool 10 minutes on prepared baking sheet. Remove to wire rack to cool completely. Store in an airtight container.

❝ These chocolate macaroons are perfect for spring with pastel jelly beans resting inside their nestlike shape. Try 'em any time of the year, and add your favorite candy pieces to the delectable confections. ❞

Dream Drops

about 2 dozen

8   egg whites
1½   cups sugar

1   cup (6 ounces) semisweet chocolate
     chips, melted

1 Preheat the oven to 250°. Beat egg whites at high speed of an electric beater until foamy. Add sugar, 1 tablespoon at a time, beating until stiff peaks form.

2 Drop by ¼-cupfuls onto parchment paper-lined baking sheets.

3 Bake at 250° for 30 minutes. Turn oven off. Let meringues stand in oven with door closed 30 minutes.

4 Spread a thin layer of chocolate on flat sides of meringues. Let stand on wax paper 2 hours.

Magical Meringue

Make meringue truly dreamy by following some basic guidelines: Let the egg whites sit at room temperature for 20 to 30 minutes before beating. Be sure your bowl and beaters are completely clean with no oil residue. Then add your sugar gradually until stiff peaks form. You'll have light-as-air meringue before you know it!

Caramel O's

about 3 dozen

1 (14-ounce) package caramel candies, unwrapped
3 tablespoons evaporated milk
1 cup chopped pecans, toasted
4 cups sweetened 3-grain apple-and-cinnamon O-shaped cereal

1 Microwave caramels in a microwave-safe 2-quart bowl at HIGH 2 minutes, stirring twice or until smooth. Stir in evaporated milk until blended. Stir in pecans and cereal.

2 Drop mixture by rounded table-spoonfuls onto a lightly greased baking sheet, and chill until firm.

Your family will call these ooey-gooey candies 'ooh-so-good'! I call them 4-ingredient fabulous!

Buckeyes

about 7 dozen

1   (16-ounce) jar creamy peanut butter
1   cup butter, softened
1½   (16-ounce) packages powdered
      sugar

2   cups (12 ounces) semisweet
      chocolate chips
2   tablespoons shortening

1 Beat peanut butter and butter at medium speed of an electric beater until blended. Gradually add powdered sugar, beating until blended.

2 Shape into 1" balls, and chill 10 minutes or until firm.

3 Microwave chocolate chips and shortening in a microwave-safe 2-quart bowl at HIGH 1½ minutes or until melted, stirring twice.

4 Use a wooden pick to dip each peanut butter ball into melted chocolate mixture, coating three-fourths of ball; place on wax paper, uncoated side up. Carefully smooth wooden pick holes. Let candies stand until chocolate hardens. Store in an airtight container in refrigerator.

"With only 5 ingredients, these divine candies are simple to make, especially when you call the neighborhood kids in to help roll and dip the balls. The hardest part will be keepin' the kids from nibbling on the peanut butter mixture."

Butterscotch-Peanut Fudge

about 2½ pounds

1 (11-ounce) package butterscotch chips
1 (14-ounce) can sweetened condensed milk
1½ cups mini marshmallows

⅔ cup chunky peanut butter
1 teaspoon vanilla extract
⅛ teaspoon salt
1 cup chopped dry-roasted peanuts

1 Heat first 3 ingredients in a small heavy saucepan over medium heat 5 to 6 minutes or until smooth, stirring constantly; remove from heat.

2 Stir in peanut butter, vanilla, and salt until blended; stir in peanuts. Pour into a buttered 9" square pan. Chill until firm; cut into squares. Store fudge in an airtight container in the refrigerator.

❝ To make this fudge even easier, microwave first 3 ingredients in a microwave-safe 2-quart bowl at HIGH 2 to 3 minutes or until melted, stirring twice. When I say easy, I mean easy! ❞

Tiger Butter

about 2 pounds

16 (1-ounce) white chocolate baking
squares, finely chopped
¾ cup creamy peanut butter

2 cups (12 ounces) semisweet
chocolate chips

1 Combine white chocolate and peanut butter in a microwave-safe 2-quart bowl. Microwave at HIGH 2½ minutes or until melted, stirring twice. Pour into a wax paper-lined 10" x 15" rimmed baking sheet, spreading evenly.

2 Microwave chocolate chips in a microwave-safe 2-quart bowl at HIGH 2½ minutes or until melted, stirring twice. Pour over white chocolate mixture; swirl gently with a knife. Chill until firm. Break into pieces. Store candy in an airtight container in refrigerator.

"This super-simple candy is a favorite at bake sales and holiday gatherings. A white chocolate and peanut butter mixture is swirled with rich, dark chocolate, making tigerlike stripes. Watch out! Everyone'll be on the hunt for more!"

METRIC EQUIVALENTS

The recipes that appear in this cookbook use the standard United States method for measuring liquid and dry or solid ingredients (teaspoons, tablespoons, and cups). The information in the following charts is provided to help cooks outside the U.S. successfully use these recipes. All equivalents are approximate.

EQUIVALENTS FOR DIFFERENT TYPES OF INGREDIENTS

A standard cup measure of a dry or solid ingredient will vary in weight depending on the type of ingredient. A standard cup of liquid is the same volume for any type of liquid. Use the following chart when converting standard cup measures to grams (weight) or milliliters (volume).

Standard Cup	Fine Powder	Grain	Granular	Liquid Solids	Liquid
	(ex. flour)	(ex. rice)	(ex. sugar)	(ex. butter)	(ex. milk)
1	140 g	150 g	190 g	200 g	240 ml
¾	105 g	113 g	143 g	150 g	180 ml
⅔	93 g	100 g	125 g	133 g	160 ml
½	70 g	75 g	95 g	100 g	120 ml
⅓	47 g	50 g	63 g	67 g	80 ml
¼	35 g	38 g	48 g	50 g	60 ml
⅛	18 g	19 g	24 g	25 g	30 ml

DRY INGREDIENTS BY WEIGHT

(To convert ounces to grams, multiply the number of ounces by 30.)

1 oz	=	¹⁄₁₆ lb	=	30 g
4 oz	=	¼ lb	=	120 g
8 oz	=	½ lb	=	240 g
12 oz	=	¾ lb	=	360 g
16 oz	=	1 lb	=	480 g

LENGTH

(To convert inches to centimeters, multiply the number of inches by 2.5.)

1 in			=	2.5 cm		
6 in	=	½ ft	=	15 cm		
12 in	=	1 ft	=	30 cm		
36 in	=	3 ft	= 1 yd =	90 cm		
40 in			=	100 cm	=	1 meter

LIQUID INGREDIENTS BY VOLUME

¼ tsp					=	1 ml		
½ tsp					=	2 ml		
1 tsp					=	5 ml		
3 tsp	=	1 tbls			= ½ fl oz =	15 ml		
		2 tbls	=	⅛ cup	= 1 fl oz =	30 ml		
		4 tbls	=	¼ cup	= 2 fl oz =	60 ml		
		5⅓ tbls	=	⅓ cup	= 3 fl oz =	80 ml		
		8 tbls	=	½ cup	= 4 fl oz =	120 ml		
		10⅔ tbls	=	⅔ cup	= 5 fl oz =	160 ml		
		12 tbls	=	¾ cup	= 6 fl oz =	180 ml		
		16 tbls	=	1 cup	= 8 fl oz =	240 ml		
		1 pt	=	2 cups	= 16 fl oz =	480 ml		
		1 qt	=	4 cups	= 32 fl oz =	960 ml		
					33 fl oz =	1000 ml	=	1 liter

COOKING/OVEN TEMPERATURES

	Fahrenheit	Celsius	Gas Mark
Freeze Water	32° F	0° C	
Room Temperature	68° F	20° C	
Boil Water	212° F	100° C	
Bake	325° F	160° C	3
	350° F	180° C	4
	375° F	190° C	5
	400° F	200° C	6
	425° F	220° C	7
	450° F	230° C	8
Broil			Grill

Index